BUT

STILL

THEY

SING

J.F. RIORDAN

Paperback: 978-0-8253-1033-1
ebook: 978-0-8253-0911-3

For inquiries about volume orders, please contact:

Beaufort Books
sales@beaufortbooks.com

Published in the United States by Beaufort Books
www.beaufortbooks.com

Distributed by Midpoint Trade Books,
a division of Independent Publishers Group
www.midpointtrade.com
www.ipgbook.com

Printed in the United States of America

Cover Design by Michael Short
Interior by Thunder Mountain Design, and Mark Karis
Cover photo: Sergei Kornilev/Shutterstock.com

With love to my new cast of girls

(in order of appearance)

Charlotte

Sophie

Emilia

Sahar

Tess

&

Claire

Table of Contents

They Sing ✤

Every morning in the dark, my prayer comes in silence. Or rather, it comes in my silence amid the conversations of others: the hundreds—possibly thousands—of geese calling at sunrise; the turkeys having another of their frequent family squabbles; the robins in their distinctive sweet monotony; the sparrows and the chickadees, each with their own language of song; the owls calling their last sleepy goodnights. Meanwhile, the raccoon slowly and silently ambles across the open lawn and up the tree trunk to bed.

The soft sleeping breath of dog one; the impatiently waiting breath of dog two; and the intense watchfulness of the puppy who sits at the window to see, hear, and smell the lives of others, these are the sounds of my prayer. This morning noise is the sound of life, of the world.

The traffic sounds that rise from the valley will come soon, too, but not yet. For now, there are just these other lives among us, busily, and with unknown degrees of self-awareness, going about the hard work of living. If they worry—and I think the garter snake we encountered in the orchard yesterday was damn worried—they don't sit around and wallow in it. They don't have time for self pity. They have to eat, and get where they have to be, and find a mate, and feed their young, and elude homicidal neighbors. Every decision they make is life or death. It's a lot. It is, frankly, more than I have to worry about, and probably more important. But they start each morning by raising their voices.

I don't know that it's cheer. Who can say? But it is life affirming. It's a statement of presence, of vitality, perhaps of territory, perhaps of love.

Life is hard and may be over before the sun sets.

But still, they sing.

(But still they sing.)

Menagerie ✤

We were walking the dogs the other night, and we saw something ahead of us in the road. The sun was going down, and it was shining in our eyes. "What is that?" my husband asked. "Is it an animal?"

He held the dogs while I went up to see. It was a tiny black kitten, sitting in the middle of the road. At first, I thought its eyes were not yet open, but as I peered into its face, I had the terrifying thought that perhaps it had no eyes at all. But no. Its eyes were mercifully there but glued shut with gunk.

I picked it up reluctantly, thinking of fleas, and cuddled it against my sweatshirt while my husband took the dogs and continued on the walk, figuring that their feelings toward the kitten might not be especially altruistic. The kitten and I went home.

I dabbed warm water on his eyes with a paper towel and wiped away the crust that was keeping them shut. He had been completely blinded, but now his eyes were open.

I found some powdered milk in the pantry and mixed it with warm water and brown sugar, and he lapped it up, trying, as puppy Auggie does, to put his feet into it.

Out in the country at our cottage, the township has no contract with the local humane society, so the Sheriff's department contacted an emergency number, and somebody from the humane society called me back. They wouldn't pick up. We would have to bring him in.

By now he was getting lively and didn't want to be held, but I was afraid he would disappear under the porch or a bush, and we wouldn't find him again. When the dogs arrived, the kitten stood on my shoulder, hissing and spitting. Moses just looked puzzled. Pete and Auggie didn't even notice him.

We drove him to the humane society, where nice people took him in, assured us that he wasn't seriously ill, and made us sign a statement that he didn't belong to us. "What's his name?" asked the woman.

"Doskar," I said. "Felix," said my husband.

We missed the sunset, which had been the whole reason we had gone to the cottage, but we didn't really mind. That kitten had a lucky, lucky day. I doubt he would have survived the night, blind, in the woods, with raccoons and foxes and coyotes, swamps to get stuck in, water to fall into. I can't help worrying about what happened to his littermates.

Every time we left the house this week, we found ourselves looking for kittens in the road. Hope they are safe somewhere, and warm.

Not With A Bang, ✳
But A Tote Bag

I seem to recall an essay by Ralph Waldo Emerson in which he predicts that the world will be subsumed not by fire or flood, but by an overwhelming mound of common pins. It hasn't happened so far, but that may be because we have shifted the cultural weight, as it were, to a far more voluminous enemy: the tote bag.

My husband is on the festival circuit. He goes to exotic and beautiful places like Maui and Aspen, cavorting with celebrities and beautiful people while I stay home with the dogs. It's not as bad as it sounds, really, and it has the advantage of enhancing spousal appreciation, but it does have a curious byproduct. Every time he returns, he presents me with a tote bag.

Tote bags are nothing new. They have been the mainstays of museum gift shops and the low-cost premium for subscriptions to magazines and public television for decades. Environmentalists made them important by urging us to pile our groceries into their bacteria-infested depths week after week rather than wounding the earth with the clean, fresh, disposability of plastic or paper grocery bags.

I love the earth. But I have questions about tote bags.

I have never had a statement handbag, but then, I live in

the Midwest, where things like that are considered ostentatious. I do find, however, almost against my will, that I have begun to select the tote bag I want depending on where I'm going and who I will be seeing. There is a hierarchy to tote bags that is more subtle than the kind of car you drive. Tote bags can brag without your ever having to say a word. They are signaling mechanisms to announce your affiliations.

The local grocery store gives out a flimsy, paper-thin canvas wine bag when you purchase more than one bottle. It's okay if you leave that one behind at your friend's house. I have a beautiful well-made canvas bag with a painting of the Flatiron Building that I purchased in a museum gift shop. It is sturdy enough to carry books and signals my cultural sophistication. This may have slightly more cachet than the thin fabric WNYC tote that seems to suggest that I am a donor (I am not) or that I am part of the East Coast intelligentsia (I am most definitely not). I have a bag from the American Enterprise Institute, proving that I am "Fighting for Freedom, Opportunity, Enterprise." That sounds nice. The TaxPayers' Alliance signals my support for fiscal restraint, and the Hoover Institution is a nice way of encouraging people to enquire whether I have met Milton Friedman or George Shultz. I have bags from book conferences that suggest my writing bona fides. I have one that declares "We Can Change the World," a claim whose sincerity I don't doubt, but about whose particulars I am somewhat skeptical. Perhaps my favorite is my niece's gift, a utilitarian lightweight "Totes Ma Goats" bag in which I carry my own books for publicity events.

But of all the tote bags, the most exclusive are those

presented as swag to attendees of various high-level conferences, like the Aspen Ideas Festival. We now have three or four Aspen tote bags. One is beautifully made from military grade canvas with leather handles and represents philanthropy to a veterans group. A bag from an exclusive corporate philanthropic retreat has a lovely, insulated pocket underneath to carry your properly chilled bottle of New Zealand sauvignon blanc or possibly a can of bug spray that wouldn't mix well with the potato salad.

Does Davos have a tote bag, I wonder? Do Davos attendees ever do anything that requires the use of a tote bag? Or do they bring them home as a bonus gift to their nannies?

As my husband's spoils of conquest accumulate in the hall closet, and the door becomes harder to close, I have begun to feel the need for some form of triage. How many tote bags does one family require? I ought to sort through, choose the most exclusive, and chuck the rest, but I'll probably keep the nice plastic one from the now-defunct local bookstore. It's easy to disinfect.

Originally published in *The Weekly Standard,* September 26, 2018.

✤ Sleepless

I have a lot on my mind: an unfinished and recalcitrant book, the usual tribulations of book sales—or lack thereof—a family reunion that includes children, five dogs, and one bathroom at our lake cottage, and a baby shower focused on the joy of the occasion, but whose logistics are daunting.

In case anyone doubts the (self-imposed) complexities of my life, I have three big dogs whose various health needs have led me to commit to giving them homemade dog food, and the coming family visits suggest that preparing eight days of dog food in advance might be advisable. There's a full day's work, not including the scramble to find affordable meat for them. It's a nuisance, but the dogs are healthy, vital, and utterly unappreciative.

I'm not sleeping well.

I defy myself in my wakefulness: I will not do laundry in the middle of the night. I just poured myself a bourbon at two a.m., which violates my own protocol, but an emergency method of acquiring some sleep before a day with many tasks.

Even in the depths of the night, the sky here is brighter than the trees, and the abstract pattern of their leaves against the pale night surrounds and engulfs the house. I lie on the couch in our library and am consoled by the sky. The dogs breathe; Pete fast and shallow as if he is racing; Moses deep and sonorant. Both follow me in my restless wanderings through the house, and we share our love and our wakefulness. Auggie, in his youth, sleeps through.

I found Pete around midnight, curled up in an odd place on the kitchen floor. Yesterday morning, I found him lying among the piles (no, mountains: two houses, visitors, bed linens, beach towels, clothing) of sorted laundry, far from his sleeping family. I wonder whether he still seeks solitude, as in his youth, or whether he is actually lost, befuddled by deafness and blindness.

Pete has much joy in life. He eats with gusto, he runs and romps. He protects his interests. He polices his younger brothers. But he is an old dog, and his quiet demeanor means he is easily pushed aside by the exigencies of the moment, and each day I resolve to spend time with Pete that is only his. Each day I fall short.

Whose kid is playing booming bass on his car stereo at three a.m. on our sleepy rural road?

I get up to start a load of laundry.

I am awake because my dreams were of my father's death: explicit; agonizing. I rose from our bed and went to where my stirrings would not disturb my hardworking husband. Moses smells my tears and licks my face.

I tell myself that my troubles are small. The world is filled with tragedies and pain, and my life is easy, rich, and full. But still, it is an act of will to find the right messaging for my troubled mind. I have a good life, it's true. But even so, grief holds hard on a heavy heart.

Adventures in Travel

I have a new set of socket wrenches. If you knew me well, you might not be completely surprised, but nevertheless, I can pretty safely say that I have never had a set of socket wrenches before.

It had been an event-filled weekend, complete with the failure of my car in a strange town, a commitment to a public appearance at a book festival, the transfer of three dogs into a rental car, four ferry rides, and a memorably unpleasant trip home, mostly from dog-related incidents.

I sold a lot of books, though.

The upshot was that the next day, I needed to return the rental car back to its home base 160 miles away. I called my sixth-grade classmate and announced that I was about to impose on our friendship.

We travel well together. She often accompanies me on my various book-related jaunts, and we always have fun. With her usual grace, she agreed to cancel her plans and follow me up north in case my car was not ready.

As it turned out, the car was not in a state to be driven and was not worth a new transmission. We left it there and decided to make the most of our trip. My friend shopped. I watched the Brewers' game at a brew pub. We met up afterward and headed home.

It had been raining off and on all day, but about this time, it began to come down in straight sheets. We had a long drive ahead of us, but we slowed down and drove cautiously. We were making good time, almost to Green Bay, when the engine light came on. "It's probably an air filter or something," I said. But then the engine power began to fail, and warning lights promising dire consequences lit up all over the dashboard.

The rain made it difficult to see, but we made it to the closest oasis, which was the usual roadside combination gas station and quickie mart. My friend called her husband. "It's done this before. You probably should disconnect the battery and reset the computer," he added helpfully. We looked at each other in silence.

"Go inside," coached my friend's husband, "and see if they have a wrench." It seemed more likely that they would have warmed-over hot dogs and hazelnut creamer, but dutifully, I went inside to see. The closest things they had to a wrench were a Green Bay Packers bottle opener and one of those pop-up tire gauges that never work.

Unencumbered by tools of any kind—although I was secretly tempted by the store's display of cheeseheads—we waited impatiently in the car as the rain poured down, hoping the engine would reset itself and we could proceed. Ultimately, it did. We set off again.

The rainstorm was of the monsoon variety, and my friend was nervous about driving. I offered to take the wheel, so she pulled over on the entrance ramp, and we performed a quick change. Neither of us is in the first bloom of youth, and my friend had loosened the top of her jeans in order to be more comfortable on the ride. As she ran around the car, the jeans began a slow slide downward. Soaked to the skin, we began laughing hysterically, driving down the road. My friend's husband was on the phone. "What's all that cackling?"

We made it another twenty miles before the engine light came on again, and we knew it was a matter of minutes before we completely lost power. This time, we were close to a truck stop. The rain was coming down as hard as ever. More hopeful this time, I went inside to see whether there was a tool we could use to disconnect the battery. I won't go into the process of taking pictures of the battery connection, and of the available tools, and texting them to friend's husband. We were in the middle of rural Wisconsin, and the signal wasn't good, so finally, I made an executive decision. I splurged on a $9.99 set of socket wrenches.

I ran back through the rain, got into the car, tore off the plastic wrapper, and opened the case. They were things of beauty, lined up according to size. Metric in one row; English in the other. They had their own perfect little niches for each socket, and three different socket wrench attachment thingies. They were pristine and shiny, and I felt oddly pleased by them. All this for $9.99.

"What can't I touch while I'm taking the battery cable off?" I asked, but the phone signal had gone dead.

Abandoned by technology, we opened the hood and stared into the engine compartment. The battery was accessible, right in the front. Feeling like Tom Hanks in *Apollo 13*, I rested the socket wrench case on the front of the car and tested to find the right size socket. My friend's husband had been right; it was a ten millimeter. Battery cable disconnected and re-attached without incident, the car started up without a warning light.

Still fairly wet despite our raincoats and hoods, we drove home the rest of the way in the pouring rain, singing songs from our childhood, cloaked in a heady sense of accomplishment. Friend's husband, waiting in his pickup with the trailer attached, just in case, met us in the parking lot of a Wal-Mart, and we followed him home.

To be perfectly clear, I understand that removing a battery cable requires neither brilliance nor expertise. But everything in life is about context. For me, it was an act of derring-do. I had stared adversity in the face and won.

This morning I sat at the kitchen counter, drinking coffee and regarding my new set of wrenches with a warm sense of pride. It's unlikely I'll ever use them again, but they will look nice neatly settled in the trunk of the new car I'm going to have to buy. Some people have souvenir cheeseheads. I have souvenir wrenches.

Originally published in *The Weekly Standard,* October 24, 2018.

❖ Unfinished Business

I began working on the stone path along side our house last year, but I'd been thinking about it for much longer than that. Our house is in the woods, which, while lovely, makes it difficult to grow grass, particularly since I refuse to use any chemicals that could be unhealthy for the dogs, or our well water, or for the trout stream at the bottom of our hill. Consequently, in a neighborhood with splendid green lawns that would put a golf course to shame, we have weeds and mud. We also have three large dogs whose ramblings, scramblings, and various activities discourage thriving plants.

Winter, when the snow has fallen, is a reprieve, but in the transitional periods, when there's rain and mud, I fight a tedious battle with muddy dogs, floors, bedding, and walls. It's not my preference, really, but it's that or squalor.

And people wonder why I love winter.

In any case, fed up, I finally bestirred myself last year to build a stone path around the house where the worst of the mud is. My decision to start had nothing to do, I'm sure, with the approaching deadline for the completion of my novel, or my writer's block, or the peculiar urges for home projects that come upon me when I should be writing. I watched to see where the dogs had made their path and went to the quarry to order stone.

My plans were for a rustic path—not a pristine suburban one, but a casual, old fashioned meandering of stone that wraps around the house and meets our terrace in back.

The stones were local limestone—large, flat, heavy, and uneven—and cutting out the soil to make them lay flat was painstaking work. Drenched in insect repellent and armed with podcasts about the Constitution and *Chapter A Day* broadcasts of my own book, I sat on the ground like a child with my triangular digging tool and hacked away at the clay soil, lifting each stone again and again to make sure the ground underneath accommodated its shape. They were large stones, and I found I could lay only about three or four a day before my energy gave out. But gradually the path wound its erratic way down the side of the house from the kitchen patio and began to curve around to meet the broad, stone terrace at the back.

I have a personal flaw that kicks in from time to time, which is a compulsion to complete something past exhaustion. I'm not completely sure of the factors that contribute to the creation of these personal storms, but when they come together, I am driven by them, occasionally to my detriment. They are more frenzy than conscientiousness. I was in one of these fevers when I carried and began to maneuver a particularly large and heavy slab of rock. It was almost three feet long and a foot and half wide, and it was heavy. I wrestled it into my grasp and carried it the thirty feet or so to where I was working. I had already created a roughly cut space in the soil for it and planned to place it, then cut around it to make it fit. I plunked it down, only a few inches from where it was supposed to go, did my work, and then, with all my strength, lifted the edge to drag it into place. Somehow, when I dropped it, I missed the right spot. It dropped onto the stone nearby, with my thumb in between.

That was a year ago last July. I still dream of the splendid vanilla frozen custard on a waffle cone I bought myself as consolation on the way home from the emergency room with a broken thumb. This is September. The path is unfinished. The remaining stone is still stacked at the edge of the driveway and beginning to grow moss. Another winter looms, and another muddy spring. I've been reluctant to break another something, but I realize that I have to get the blasted thing finished. It's a pandemic. I have time. I tell myself that if I put down just one stone a day, I can be finished before the snow falls. But I know that the hassle of getting ready to do the job and of cleaning up afterward means that I will feel compelled to do more than one. I have promised myself that this week I will start.

Did I mention I've begun a new novel?

The Souls Of Our Selves

I have been reading several books by Jane Goodall, who is a hero of mine. She describes with great clarity the condescension and arrogance of the scientific world as she was beginning her career. But it is the personalities of her animal acquaintances—friendships—that captivate me. Not because I am surprised by the depth and complexity of the animals' emotions, but because humanity has for so long doubted their existence.

Until Ms. Goodall's work, I wonder whether anyone even remotely involved in these scientific inquiries had ever shared a home with a dog or cat, although René Descartes, who famously said that animals were soulless machines unable to feel pain, also dissected his wife's dog.

My husband is away for a few days, and the house has felt empty without him. But I sleep well out here in the country, buffered somewhat by several glasses of wine and protected by my two big German Shepherds who sleep on the bed with me. They shift positions during the night. At one point, young Eli crept up next to me and put his face next to mine, and I was comforted by his gentle snores, which sounded like purring. Later, Auggie, perhaps jealous, moved up and put his head on the pillow on the other side, and I was forced to shift my body diagonally to find a place to put my legs. It wasn't quite comfortable, but I liked it anyway, surrounded by these big, fierce animals who love me.

For most of my life it has been fashionable among scientists to lecture animal lovers about the emotional inadequacy of our fellow creatures. We were told that dogs, for example, don't really love us, but merely respond out of self-interest to the pack leader who will give them food. Dogs' behaviors can be misinterpreted by us—and they often are by doting but careless owners—but anyone who's ever spent five minutes with a dog knows that they absolutely do express love. Fortunately, that notion of human superiority is no longer scientifically accepted.

I often wonder what my dogs are thinking and how they perceive the world, but I have no doubt of their feelings. I know their joy, their guilt, their disappointment, and most definitely their love. I can read the emotion on their faces and in their body language, and it is as clear as with any human.

Auggie is particularly communicative, because he is mature and has learned the meanings of my words and how to speak with gestures. His eyes express his sensitive nature, and when he is hurt by too much attention shown to Eli, they droop with heartbreaking sadness. They sparkle with mischief and anticipation as he watches my face for permission to run out and play. They are deep and searching as he longs for words to explain to me that the braunschweiger is right there on the kitchen counter and it would be delicious. These are not my projections. People who barely know him comment on his expressions and interpret them correctly and without context.

"He looks sad; he wants something; he's excited; he loves you."

Eli, still a two-year-old giant puppy, has less subtlety, but his feelings are intense. His remorse when he was sick, couldn't wake me, and made a mistake in the house—which for a German Shepherd is a mortal sin—was heartbreaking. It was impossible to blame him or to be angry.

Now we are seeing studies about animal altruism, about the shifts in their calls to reflect their surroundings, about their grief for their dead, about their terror of the abattoir. In a world shaken by a new awareness of its cruelty to the "other," we continue to deny and neglect the reality that is before our eyes daily.

Last week I passed a dead squirrel by the side of the road, and in the rearview mirror, I saw his living friend sniffing and touching him in hopes he could be roused.

Descartes be damned. Those of us who have animals in our homes and our lives know the truth: they are not children of a lesser God, but of the very same God, and they deserve to share the same status in His beloved creation.

Animals have souls. They are individuals. Their longings, loves, and fears are as palpable and real as ours. When we ignore this reality, we are the perpetrators of sin, putting not just animals, but our selves and our souls in grave peril.

Spring and All

It is the time of year when life blooms. The frogs are singing, the geese are still flying overhead to the place where they will spend the night. The robins chirrup the call that means, to me, dawn and dusk. But if I stand in my driveway, with the dogs lying still, I can hear things growing. Literally. There is a rustle in the woods that does not come from an animal's movement. It is the slow, steady creep of leaves and stems and flowers, finding their place in the light and air.

I am nostalgic with memories of childhood spring concerts, graduations, proms, life events. The soft green nascence of leaves and flowers, the scent of bloom, the memory of love, of longing. Spring smells of all these things.

My job is ending. I don't know when I will work again, but my husband has declared it a day of liberation. We drink old champagne, the sound of birds and lawn mowers in the background, the birds singing their ancient, unchanging songs. I hear the robins, the cardinals, the sparrows, the meadowlarks, the woodpeckers, and the phoebes. The bird songs are mixed with the soft insistence of puppy Auggie, whining under his breath that I should pay attention to him, to his green ball.

The lilies of the valley are still coiled in tight rolls, waiting to unfold. The bluebells have begun to bloom, but they have not yet burst into riot. The narcissi spill their scent upon the air. The peonies push their red shoots up, and I look for a careful placement of the metal rings that will keep their blooms from lying on the ground a few weeks hence. I dream of them all winter, of their exuberant, joyous explosion.

The turkeys, no longer visible on the ground in the woods, rise up from green bowers into their now hidden roosts. The deer chuff among the trees as they browse, but the green leaves hide their movement. A big raccoon makes her cumbersome way down a tall tree to begin her nighttime rambles.

It is spring. The world is poised. A great writer died last night, and I feel the world's aftershocks. We are smaller now without him.

Nevertheless, this old song sings. The frogs, the geese, the robins, the rustling leaves. It is soft-scented and sweet.

The world goes on, beautiful and ruthless. We watch, worn, enchanted, hopeful, but powerless to change the slow, hard progress of life.

✳ Old Joys

I wonder: am I the only one who finds it painful to look at photos? I see something from a particular day, and I think about what a beautiful day it was, and how filled with joy, and then I realize that it's gone forever. What is this new melancholy? Is it age? Is it the remnants of grief? Is it the strange, pandemic-induced sense of being an old woman already, borne of almost a year of living in my own house, going from bed, to desk, to chair, to the edge of the property line, barely stirring. No concerts, no plays, no cheerful lunches with friends. I feel that I am living the life of an 85-year-old.

Still, I live a beautiful life. My snug house sits on a ridge, and the big windows at the back look east into a valley of trees, artesian springs, and many animals. I can see the sunrise in the morning and, in the afternoon, the slow fading of the light into gold, then rose, then the crystalline blue of the winter sky. There is a fire in the fireplace, the warm chaos of three happy dogs. Outside in the dark of pre-dawn, there are deer at the bottom of the hill, eating the seeds and nuts I put out for them during this spell of bitter cold. Distant blue mountains at the horizon are towering columns of mist rising from Lake Michigan.

I can hear the dogs moving as my husband stirs. I have no serious complaints in life, but at the same time, I am not without desires, or ambition. I think longing for things is a fine state to be in.

I am at an age when I am losing the leading edge of people in my life. Our parents are gone, and this year, my godmother, and a kind elderly neighbor. My husband and I joke grimly that we are next. My mother's oldest friend and her twin sister have become my friends over the years, and they just turned ninety. Their varying attitudes about life seem to reflect their varying states of health. Or is it the other way around?

Which brings me back to the photos of the three of us together more than thirty years ago. I, young, slim, and smiling, they in robust and cheerful middle age. Come to think of it, my age now. I feel a deep sense of loss when I see these photos. Not of my youth, as such. Nor of theirs. But for the days of the long horizon, of good health taken for granted, of dreams unfulfilled, but hoped for.

The photos remind me of what I have lost. It is better, I believe, to focus on the present, to savor today's joys, to enjoy what has been achieved, and hold to hopes for the future. To look back is to grieve.

So, is that what photos are for?

❋ The Paradox of Inspiration

My father was the proverbial rocket scientist. He had more than 120 patents on everything from missile guidance systems, to seals for airplane windows, to antilock braking systems. I can remember, as a little girl, waking up and being told by my mother to be quiet because my father was sleeping. He had awakened with an idea and worked all night on a new invention.

As a writer, I am often asked about my inspiration. It's a difficult question to answer, because it is so complex and mysterious, but I have come to accept certain truths about the process, even though they are somewhat contradictory. I can't call them rules, because that is too restrictive, and inspiration needs freedom. But they are principles that are helpful to acknowledge in all their unpredictable glory.

The first fundamental about inspiration is that you have to earn it. Inspiration rarely comes when you aren't working. It comes while you have been working and working hard. I can't expect to spend days procrastinating and then suddenly have a vision of an intact scene for a novel come into my head. Usually, I have to be following a settled discipline of early risings, long hours of concerted—perhaps merely workmanlike—writing for days, or possibly weeks. I some-times feel that inspiration is a bit like the Peanuts character Linus and his sincere pumpkin patch. Like the Great Pumpkin, the Muse only visits those who have earned the privilege.

Once you have established a rhythm in your work, you reach a state of flow that has both facility and creativity. Pieces seem to fit together with ease, and every knot is easily untied. This is the core of the writing process and a principle that every creative discipline seems to share: do the work, and the work will do itself. You have to build the scaffolding of discipline as the underlying structure of your work.

The second fundamental is that you have to keep an open heart. I had been in a particularly productive writing cycle, and everything had been flowing. One night I was driving home from some event, the kind of cocktail party where everyone wears name tags: boring, cheerless, and obligatory. There was snow falling, and I was almost home when suddenly a voice came into my head, speaking in the first person. I raced home to write it down, standing at the kitchen counter without even taking my coat off.

The next morning, I looked at what I had written. It was compelling, complete, and real, but uncomfortably intense. It was also odd, different from anything else I had written, and it didn't really fit with the rest of the book. Reluctantly, instead of using it, I set it aside, hoping it might work for some other project.

Then, my muse went dark. Everything stopped. I couldn't write. I couldn't advance the plot of my story. I couldn't find the thread. I sat at my desk in the dark every morning, and nothing happened. Finally, acknowledging defeat, I gave up, set everything aside to brew, and went about my life. Weeks later, on a snowy January morning, I stood barefoot at my open door looking out over the woods and suddenly saw where that abandoned voice fit. It did belong in the novel, and I knew exactly where. I sat down then and there and from that moment on, the story began to move again.

By shutting down my inspiration, I had shut down the whole process. I hadn't listened. Meanwhile, my subconscious had been wrestling with the problem and searching for a solution. Like stargazing, where you have to look away from something to fully see it, inspiration can require you to look away from your work. My father, who had daily been struggling to find the answer to some problem, would wake up one night knowing the solution.

And that's the contradiction to the first principle. Inspiration comes when you are working, but sometimes you have to stop working in order to find it. The key is that when you stop, it has to be the right kind of procrastination.

Procrastination has two forms: there is the procrastination that comes from laziness or self-indulgence, when you want to sleep a little longer, buy things online, or waste an hour on Twitter. But there's also a form of procrastination that is a kind of gestation period, when, like Jacob wrestling the angel, your subconscious is struggling to solve a problem. If you are honest with yourself, you know which is which. You look away to see the star. You need to refuse the indulgence but honor the gestation.

I heard an interview a while back with a songwriter. She

spoke of a river of inspiration flowing over her head that she could reach into and pull down the music. She believed that certain ideas are there just for you, but if you don't accept them, they are given to someone else. That idea of the river is appealing. But it is interesting that she, too, was speaking of being receptive to the inspiration, as if the inspiration is something outside yourself. If you reject it—if you don't keep an open heart—you lose it, and someone else is chosen.

It isn't a predictable or even a logical process. Being chosen isn't a given. You have to make yourself ready to be chosen by doing the work, by showing up at your desk every day, by building the discipline necessary to turn the inspiration into something worth reading. Even in its contradictions, the process seems to be universal. Make yourself worthy, and when you stop to listen, the inspiration will come.

Originally published in the online magazine, *Books for Women; Women Writers, Women's Books*, February 24, 2019.

Donald Hall: A Remembrance

few weeks ago, I received a printed postcard in the mail, addressed to "Correspondent of Donald Hall". In a few brief lines it announced that Don had been diagnosed with cancer and would no longer be able to read or answer any letters.

I never met Donald Hall. But our lives crossed paths in ways that profoundly influenced me.

My piano teacher was a kindly man named Reuel Kenyon. I remember him telling my mother one day that his daughter, Jane, then an unknown student, was getting married to a university professor. At that same time, my older brother was one of Donald Hall's students at University of Michigan.

I was a very little girl, but my brother came home and read to me the poetry he was studying in Hall's classes. He taught me about his teacher's passion for the ancient, stopped rhythms in "Baa, Baa Black Sheep," and "Hark! Hark! The dogs do bark." He read many things to me that he had encountered in class, but he most particularly loved the poetry of Theodore Roethke, a friend and colleague of his professor's. At Hall's suggestion, my brother bought a Caedmon recording of Roethke reading his works, and we would listen to it again and again until we both knew all the poems by heart. To this day those words are embedded on my heart and brain, and I feel that they belong particularly to me, all because of Donald Hall's passion for them.

Eventually, I acquired other recordings of poets reading their work, and the power and value of memorizing their poetry makes it baffling to me that memorization is so sneered at by modern teachers. These things in my life have been a tremendous gift, building the music and rhythms that have become the roots of my own writing, and offering a deeply personal library that is always accessible. At unexpected moments, snippets of lines of poetry suddenly come to mind, perfectly *a propos*, and then the cascade of verses flows, unbidden, to enrich an ordinary conversation.

String Too Short to be Saved was the first book of Donald Hall's that I bought—or perhaps, was given—back when I was in college. It's still here on my shelves, along with all his other books.

While I was in college, I also cut out and saved "Polonius's Advice to Poets." Its dry wit still resonates. I have read that essay so many times over the years that I have come to use some of its lines as stock phrases that recur in my daily conversations. "My sister's funeral was boring, but I got a poem out of it;" the mockery of (badly) translated poetry, "the bamboo under the mountain-color mountain;" and most important, "Remember what matters." I did not remember Polonius's advice to "write to poets and critics you admire, and some will write you back," but apparently internalized it all the same. (The same college friend who probably gave me

String Too Short also gave me that essay and introduced me to baseball—another life-altering gift.)

Over the years, I read and enjoyed all of Hall's books, including his poetry, and that of his late wife, the sorrowful and acerbic poet, Jane Kenyon. His account of her death, *The Best Day the Worst Day: Life with Jane Kenyon,* is a haunting statement of loss.

One day, after tucking one of Donald Hall's books into a shelf in my office, I went online and happened upon the essay, "Between Solitude and Loneliness." I had read the first few paragraphs before I suddenly saw his byline. Perhaps I felt I already knew Donald Hall, but something at that moment compelled me to write to him.

"I don't know whether it will mean anything to you," I wrote, "but I wanted to tell you that even though you were never actually my teacher, your passion for words profoundly influenced me and my life, and for that I am genuinely grateful."

The letter sat on the kitchen table for some time before my husband—who is valuable in this way—asked when I was going to send it. I had no address, but I knew the name of Donald Hall's farm and that he lived in New Hampshire, so I spent a leisurely morning stalking him online, using Google Earth to locate the farm and trying to read the address on the mailbox. I could not, but it was time to move on, so I went to the UPS office anyway. "We don't have this address on file," they said. "Just send it," I told them. "They'll know."

And then, in a gesture that all writers will recognize, I threw my fate into the winds and got on with my life.

About ten days later, I opened the mailbox and felt a jolt

and a thrill to see an envelope with a return address in New Hampshire. It was from Donald Hall.

We began what became, sadly, a correspondence of only a few months. He told me about the first publication of *String Too Short to be Saved*, crediting Roger Angell for publishing the first few chapters in *The New Yorker*, we wrote about our drinking habits—he permitted himself two Manhattans a week—and he consoled me about the frustrations of being an unknown writer, saying, "I suppose being called a regional writer is as bad as being called 'a Robert Frost imitator.'"

He wrote about the death of my old piano teacher, Jane's father. "Jane had flown from New Hampshire to Michigan to visit her mother, and they were sorting through old things in the house, and late in the day, her mother Polly said, 'Let evening come.'" Her three words started one of Jane Kenyon's most powerful poems. "Twilight: After Haying," also about the death of her father, was, he said, one his favorites. "But," he said, "I have many favorites."

His letters must have been dictated. They had a chatty quality, but he clearly read them before they were sent and added corrections and additions with a pen. "I don't like much of the poetry that gets published these days either, to begin with because the poems do not make a noise when read aloud! Sound is the way in!"

Hall, himself, was a gifted reader, and his sonorous lines echo on numerous recordings. He admired the way "Ted Roethke and Dylan" read their poems. "I adored reading aloud," he wrote, "and I miss it a lot. I think Seamus read aloud well. I heard him three or four times and knew him a bit. Horrid that he died at a mere seventy-three."

He chastised me about my bad handwriting, "I have to tell you that your address on the envelope is unreadable," and talked about writing *String Too Short to be Saved,* offering a glimpse of his work ethic.

> That year in the village of Thaxted … it was the third bit of writing I did in the day. Every morning I made coffee and worked on poems in the kitchen first thing in the day. Mid-day I looked at letters and wrote book reviews for *The New Statesman* and *Encounter,* and then at around tea time I took a pad of paper up to the Music Room. (There was a gorgeous late fourteenth century house we lived in that year! It was a wonderful year. Kirby fed the baby Philippa straight to the cup. At the end of the year we rented a car and drove to Rome and I interviewed Ezra Pound.) But every afternoon I wrote *String.* My first prose book. I learned how to write prose by writing it.

He was looking forward to a new great grandchild and the publication this fall of his new book of essays, *A Carnival of Losses, Notes Nearing Ninety.* "In my eighties," he wrote me, "I had to give up writing poems, but I was lucky to be able still to write prose. Nobody in his or her mid-eighties has ever written a good poem, alas. Poetry is too erotic."

Our correspondence was starting to build a rhythm when the postcard arrived. It was hard to know the right thing to do in the face of its message, but it seemed wrong not to respond at all.

"Even if this is just a statement to the universe," I wrote, "I need to say that you are in my thoughts, that I pray for you, and that your work has great meaning to me and to the world of letters. You once wrote "remember what matters." I hope that you are still fighting, because struggling is life. Your work matters. And all of those things that have mattered to you have touched my life through your writing. Thank you for that."

I shall always be grateful.

❖

Originally published in *The Weekly Standard*, July 2, 2018.

Words for the Newlyweds

I would like to point out to those who don't know me that I am not merely an aunt, but that I am in fact, The Sainted Aunt. In that role I would like to offer some small pieces of advice, which the bride and groom probably won't hear today or remember later.

Never mind.

Madeleine L'Engle is best known for her science-fiction children's books. But she was also a prolific essayist. One day while reading something of hers about creativity, one sentence brought me up short.

It was this: Love isn't an emotion. It's a policy.

That may be an odd thing to say at a wedding, but it is the secret to all relationships. Because if we base our relationships solely on how we feel, then we have the power to ignore them if we become tired, to throw them away if we can't forgive, to crush them and destroy them if we are angry.

The intense passion and devotion we feel for one another at the beginning is not an experience that continues constantly. People annoy us; they bore us; they disappoint us; they desperately hurt us; they forget to pick up their socks. So, does that mean if we aren't feeling passion, we don't love? Of course not—if it did, no human relationship would last more than a few minutes.

No. Love has its seasons of emotions that come and go, but it is, in fact a policy. It is a decision we make about commitment, about value, and for the day-to-day essence of any relationship, it determines how we treat each other in the casual exchanges of everyday life.

It is so often true that we make more effort to be civil to strangers than we do to people in our own house. Surely these people whom we love most deserve our most full effort to be kind? So, my first piece of advice is to be polite to each other. Save your best selves for each other, not for strangers. If you do that, your home will always be a place of refuge.

Life with humans—even with dogs, as any of us who loves dogs will know—also involves a lot of mistakes. And thoughtlessness. And grievous hurts. And when we are hurt, it is natural to be angry. It is an instinct of self-love and preservation. But to nurture anger is to willingly harbor a killer within your heart. George MacDonald said, "It may be infinitely less evil to murder a man than to refuse to forgive him. The former may be a moment of passion; the latter is the heart's choice. It is spiritual murder, the worst, to hate, to brood over a feeling …"

And in any relationship—especially in marriage when, at our most vulnerable, we can innocently hurt one another—it is essential to drop your pride and take your example from dogs: apologize, and then forgive, apologize and forgive, and forgive again.

If you remember only one thing today, make it forgiveness.

My last piece of advice may be, ironically, the most difficult.

We have some friends who have a very busy life. He has a very successful business; she does, too. His 93-year-old grandfather, who has the beginnings of dementia, lives with them and likes to wander out on his own to mow the lawn. They have three children, and one of them, a teenager, is seriously ill. Their life is full and busy and demanding. It can be hard. But every morning when they wake up, he says to her: how are we going to have fun today?

One of my favorite public figures is John Cleese—one of the original members of Monty Python. Think of a sort of 1970's version of Eddie Izzard. Since the days of the television show, he has gone on to a career, believe it or not, as a creativity consultant—which sounds like a sketch from the show, but it is actually perfectly true.

Cleese talks about the distinction between being serious and being solemn. He points out that you can be sitting around a table talking about the most serious things in the world: love, death, the meaning of life, great literature, and you can be laughing while you speak of them. Serious doesn't mean humorless. And you don't have to go to the circus—or the New York trapeze school—to have fun.

But laughing and finding escape can be liberating and inspiring and relationship building.

Not to mention a whole lot cheaper than psychotherapy.

Our life's landscape isn't geographical. It's human. When you are young, life is an endless horizon of years ahead. It's hard to realize how fast time goes, and how quickly the people we assume will always be here can suddenly be gone, changing the world forever. It's easy to allow the demands of every day to take up our energy and our hours. But in this, in every day, we have the essence of our lives. Our lives are only time, and, however far off the horizon seems, finite. So, take the time every day to have fun together.

For all that, marriage is serious business. To return to Madeleine L'Engle, (and I am paraphrasing) marriage is a fearful gamble, requiring risking everything of yourself. Marriage starts with love, and it is something that you must create together. And, she says, it is that creation that is part of our human calling.

So ... remember ...

Love isn't a feeling. It's a policy.

Be polite.

Apologize.

Forgive, forgive, forgive.

Have fun.

Now off you go.

From my talk at my niece's wedding.

❖ A Perfect View

I detest the details of airline travel. And I have done a lot of it. I traveled when I was an opera singer, making trips to and from Europe every six weeks or so. I travelled in my work for a foundation, often to spectacular resorts I would never be able to afford myself. But on the way to the airport, I've always had a tight little knot in my stomach and a nagging sense that I'd never be home again.

When I travelled as a singer there was some tension about whether my luggage was too heavy—I did once bring a piece of exercise equipment with me to Germany—about the ordeal of passport control—which was just inconvenient because of the long lines—and now TSA with the insane chaos of going through security—even though I have pre-check and Global Entry—and all the rest. It's just a whole lot of hoops to jump through, I guess. But there's always that moment once I've passed through security and haven't lost my ID, my phone, or my boarding pass (which I prefer on paper), when I literally breathe a sigh of relief and feel that the fun can begin.

Because I love flying. I love everything about it.

There is the sense of adventure, of course. Of flying off to make my dreams come true. Of going to meet loved ones. Of escaping the ordinary to reach some new destination with alligators, or whales, or great museums. The smell of jet exhaust reminds me with nostalgia of my first trip to Europe with my parents, the strangeness of everything, the mixture of exhaustion and exhilaration as you step out of the airport in early morning and find yourself in a new world.

I love taking off. The moment when the plane turns onto the runway and pauses while the flight attendants drone in the background, the whine of the engines, the acceleration—fast, faster, faster—until the moment of lift-off, when the small child in me cannot help whispering, "We're flying!"

And we are.

I love leaning against the bulkhead to watch the sky and the ground separate, the bump of the landing gear retracting, and that first stiff, sharp turn to head over Lake Michigan and away. I love the strange lines and details of the water, like skin, with wrinkles and pock marks sometimes, sometimes with white-crested waves, or at sunset with the shadow of the city on the blue water.

I love the smell of airline coffee in the early morning and holding the hot cup steaming in my hands, whitened with that fake cream they use. I love the buzz and burr of the unintelligible announcements from the flight deck. I love, on night flights, the pleasure of holding a glass of wine in my hands, watching the world slip away into the darkness.

But the moment I love most of all is on an overcast day, when the plane, after bumping and jogging through the currents, ascends through the cloud ceiling, and suddenly there is a gleam of sunlight. Then, as the plane breaks through the clouds, instead of gloom, there is blue sky and sunshine, the world magically transformed. The clouds seem to invite you to lounge on them in a long vista of the most beautiful scene in the world.

In this moment I feel an internal shift. My worries fall away, and my soul drifts out among the clouds. I lean back in my seat and watch, feeling that somehow, I'm in the precursor to eternity.

Remembering Pete du Pont

Ionce rode through Washington's Dupont Circle with Pete du Pont and asked him about his relationship to the admiral on the horse. I don't remember precisely what he said (looking it up now, I see they were distant cousins) so much as the airy and unassuming style of his response. It was a rare mixture of pride and delight—acknowledging that he was one of America's aristocrats, but without either vanity or condescension, as if he were sharing a joke. And that moment—perhaps particularly the delight—is how I best remember Pete du Pont.

My father was fond of the aphorism that a gentleman is someone who never insults anyone unintentionally. Pete du Pont was the quintessential gentleman. His manners were impeccable, worn with an ease that made them a perfectly natural part of who he was. He carried his intellect lightly and—despite some of the sneering nicknames used by his political opponents—his treatment of others was utterly without pretense.

I got to know him in the 2000s—long after he had left Delaware's governorship and run for president—when he was on the board of directors of a foundation where I worked. He was already in his late sixties and had a particular grace and sophistication, along with an unselfconscious boyish charm. But he was a serious person with firm values and strongly held views, and one had a profound sense of his candor and honesty. I imagine that disappointing him would not have been a happy experience. I saw the casual way he could put a rude or foolish person on notice, like a musketeer with an easy flick of the sword.

The first realization of his intelligence could be gleaned by the look in his eyes—interested, sparkling, seemingly always with a glint of humor. He asked pointed questions, he thought deeply, and he listened carefully. He treated everyone—no matter their rank or status—with the same genuineness and respect, and unlike many of his colleagues, he never assumed someone else would do the dirty work. It may seem a small thing, but in a room full of heavyweight capitalists and intellectuals, he carried other people's plates to the kitchen.

After a working lunch one day, there was a basket of cookies left at the buffet sideboard that had been judiciously avoided by health-conscious colleagues. Pete picked it up and went to each person sitting around the table, teasing and cajoling everyone to take a cookie, as if we were at a children's birthday party.

He always had a sense of fun that lightened the mood of the room he was in.

Even in an atmosphere of weighty conversations, he was the personification of *joie de vivre*, but he did not lose the thread, nor the significance, nor the serious implications of the decisions being made.

I can't say I knew him well, or that I had a deep personal

relationship with him. But from the first moment I met him, he had my respect and admiration. No matter the circumstances, or the challenges, or the demands of the occasion, he rose to meet them with cheer, integrity, and the confidence of someone who knows it will all come out right in the end.

I don't know what better qualities one could want for a life well-lived.

Originally published in the online magazine *The Bulwark*, May 10, 2021.

On The Importance Of Fairy Tales

When I was very small and just learning to read, my grandmother gave me a fat, red volume of best-loved fairy tales. I was very proud to have a grown-up book, and I was not intimidated by the size of it, only by its lack of illustration. I doubt she ever had any idea how much influence it would have on me. I lived inside that book. Through fairy tales, I absorbed the virtues and values of a moral life that were highly prized and perfectly expressed in those stories. The rules, although never explicit, were crystal clear.

1. Be kind, particularly to strangers and very odd creatures. You never know who could be a fairy in disguise.

2. Be worthy. Because goodness is rewarded one way or another.

3. Be brave—which is not the same as fearless.

4. Be patient. There are trials in life.

5. Share. Even if you have very little, allow a hungry creature—human or otherwise—to partake of your meager meal. See Rule #1.

6. There are witches, evil fairies, gnomes, trolls, and cruel stepmothers who will try to harm you, and elves who will try to trick you. Beware.

7. Be wily but be true. Put your values above risk.

8. Liars and crooks will be punished.

9. Beware of stepparents (which, if you read the news, maybe isn't such terrible advice).

10. The world is wild and cruel, but there is beauty and magic in it.

One of life's most important lessons is an undercurrent in nearly every fairy tale: be prepared to encounter evil. But— and this is key—the mere presence of evil in the world is less significant than how evil is faced. Fairy tales are filled with those who stand firm on the side of goodness, as well as with those who capitulate and meet a bad end. When faced with cruelty, the heroes of fairy tales are kind. When faced with duplicity, they are patient, wily, and clever. They persevere through great trials. They are hungry, cold, cast out, forbidden from attending the ball. But they win in the end.

Adults tend to be squeamish about the raw cruelty in fairy tales, and in this era of unhealthy over-protectiveness, there is earnest talk about damaging tender psyches. We forget that children are a curious mix of literal understanding with no capacity to grasp mortality. Death won't happen to them. Uncomplicated black-and-white rules are comprehensible. So, amidst the fascinating stories of poisoned apples, evil enchanted dogs getting their heads cut off, witches baking children into gingerbread, and cruel stepmothers leaving innocent children in the woods, young readers are able to express their fears and absorb the lessons of the world without pedantry or ambiguity.

People often focus on the princess stories, believing it is wrong to teach girls that they will be rescued by a prince. I don't think that's the message at all. I think the message is: *if you are good, and kind, and patient, you will be rewarded with love and happiness, and maybe a little bit of magic.*

The classic heroines of fairy tales, Cinderella, Snow White, and Sleeping Beauty, all endure cruelty and unfairness, but they aren't changed by it. They are lovely because they are filled with kindness and generosity of spirit. If you get caught up in their beauty—or that of the handsome prince—you miss the point. The heroines' physical appearance, and the prince's wealth and high status are metaphor. These young women have good hearts. This is why they are desirable. This is why they deserve love and the rewards of a good life.

In my experience, little girls who want to be Cinderella, want to be good as she is, not wicked, like her stepsisters. The stepsisters are sometimes depicted as being physically ugly, but their true ugliness is in their characters. They are proud, haughty, selfish, and vain, not to mention cruel. Little girls may want to be pretty, too (who doesn't?), but properly exposed to fairy tales, they internalize the real message: that beauty is inside. Wise adults refrain from imposing their own anxieties and emphasize the true lessons of these stories: what matters is how we treat others and whether we give of ourselves.

In the world of fairy tales, how we treat others is of paramount importance. A recurring theme is the necessity of being kind to strangers—human or otherwise—even the ugliest, oddest, most terrifying of them. The hungry stranger at the gate is given a bowl of porridge when food at the cottage is scarce; the trapped wild animal is gently released, even at risk to the rescuer; the demanding and ugly frog is kissed. The result is more wonderful than could have been imagined.

It worked for me.

Many years ago, I was kind to someone when I didn't always feel like it. He would call wanting to talk, and I would put my day on hold to listen, even though it was, frankly, a bit of a nuisance. We would sometimes talk for hours. I had not been kind as a means to an end. I had no inkling that he would influence things in my favor. This went on for years. One day, out of the blue, he called to tell me about an important job, one that changed my life. His recommendation got my interview. It wasn't until much later that I realized he had been the fairy at my gate, disguised as a beggar.

Again and again in fairy tales, physical appearance is shown to be deceptive; it is character that truly matters. Cruel stepmothers can be beautiful but dangerously vain. Horrifying deformities may hide a fairy. A hideous beast may hide a loving prince. In a tale like *Beauty and the Beast*, the power of love transforms the qualities of human nature, and children learn to look past superficial appearance and gruffness to the heart that beats beneath. Its message—like that of nearly every tale—is that love tames the beast in us all.

At the same time, any one of us can fall prey to greed,

selfishness, and stupidity, and this, too, is important to remember. Any wish-granting tale will caution what can happen to decent people when unexpected wealth comes their way. Or, come to think of it, any newspaper story about a lottery winner.

These stories mostly share Judeo-Christian values, but I believe that many of them pre-date Christianity. Consider the anthropological theory that legends of elves and gnomes hiding in the forest may be a memory of the interactions between modern humans and Neanderthals, who, we now know, existed contemporaneously. Fairy tale morality reflects the basic infrastructure of a healthy society. It shows an imperfect world made better or worse by the deeds of us all. And it suggests that acting with a good heart—without cruelty or rancor—will be rewarded.

There aren't all happy endings. Hans Christian Andersen's *The Little Mermaid*—which is a relatively modern tale—teaches about injustice, and envy, and trying to be what you're not. It is a tragedy as pure as Romeo and Juliet with miscommunication leading to heartbreak and death. Nevertheless, the goodness of the mermaid herself is rewarded, even if she does not win her kind (though somewhat stupid) prince.

Think about what the public discourse would be like if everyone followed the standards of fairy tales. Twitter would dissolve like a wicked witch doused with water. Immigrants and strangers would be seen as beings with hearts and souls like our own and welcomed at our gates. The hungry and afflicted would be treated with kindness and fed from our own pantries. Animals would be protected and cared for. Library books would be returned on time, even if it meant walking through storms to get there.

When I hear discussions about the dangers of fairy tales to young minds, I think about what I learned from them and take a look at the world around us.

Frankly, we could do worse.

And often do.

The Kindness of Strangers: New York Version

I was in New York for a book convention and was heading home in a very good mood. My traveling companion and I have known one another for over thirty years. We met in the theater. She always comes with me to these things and acts as my carnival barker to attract people to my booth. She's extremely good at this.

Although slightly hungover, we were reminiscing and singing show tunes on the ride to the airport. She got out at a different terminal, and for the remainder of the trip, the cab driver, who was a refugee from Afghanistan, and I had a pleasant few minutes talking about friendship. He was a nice guy, and I tipped him well. We parted with a handshake. This is a lesson: be nice to people, and they'll be nice to you. Also, get a receipt.

I was walking into the terminal when I reached into my pocket for my boarding pass, which was on my phone. My phone wasn't in my pocket. It wasn't in my handbag. It wasn't in my backpack.

It was in the cab.

You know that sickening feeling when you've lost something of value. But we all have a particular and dangerous dependency on our phones that made this loss particularly dire. How would

I call my husband to say I might be late? Or the dog sitter whose number I didn't know by heart? Does directory assistance even exist anymore? I couldn't reach my friend, only a short way away in the next terminal. Everything we need is on our phones: our TSA numbers, our insurance agent's phone, and the most intimate details of our lives. Our wallets barely matter. Did I mention it was a brand-new phone?

I checked my luggage, got a new paper boarding pass, and stood thinking about what to do. If there were any pay phones, who would I call? If I could only call the cab driver ...

An airline employee named Phil was directing the lines, and when I told him my dilemma, he handed me his phone. I wanted to call the cab company. "No. Call yourself," he told me. "The driver will hear it ringing, and at least know it's there."

So, I called myself, several times, and then went back out to the drop-off in the hope that the cab might be able to come around again. But after a few minutes of waiting, the unlikeliness of this prospect sank in. I went back inside to Phil, this time to ask if I could call the cab company. I had the receipt and the cab number. "You'll be on hold forever," he told me. But I had to try. So, Phil again handed me his phone while he continued his work with other passengers.

Then, as I waited on hold, a miracle happened: my own phone number popped up. I handed the phone to Phil to answer. It was the cab driver. He had pulled off the highway and was in the LaGuardia taxi waiting area. He couldn't just sit there, the line was moving, and he'd soon be pushed out. I needed to come immediately to get my phone. He told me to hurry. Talking fast, Phil explained that the cab area was off the airport premises and down the highway. It was a distance. I couldn't walk there, and I would really have to hurry.

I grabbed a cab as it was dropping off another passenger and told the driver the problem. Could he help me? We broke the rules about passenger pick-ups and sped off. I asked him to call my phone. Soon, we were out on the highway, driving fast, away from the airport and my checked luggage, as the two drivers argued volubly about how to get to the right place.

It had been maybe five minutes, and I was beginning to worry when we headed up an exit ramp, dodging and weaving around slower traffic as if we were in a chase scene all while the drivers continued arguing. The current driver, an African with a beautiful accent and a warm, deep voice, had a kind of other-worldly authority. The other, my kindly Afghani friend, had an almost hysterical sense of urgency. "No, no, no!" I heard him screaming into the phone. "That's not the right place! NO!"

"Listen," said the African driver calmly as he whipped around a tiny Fiat that was driving too slowly and cut in front of it. "You have to stop talking and listen to me."

The Fiat driver, a cute elderly lady with wild, curly hair, flipped us off.

We squeezed past a Hyundai with inches to spare and squealed around the corner before the light changed.

The drivers, having apparently reached some kind of concord, hung up. I knew we were close, but I hadn't understood what they were talking about. It felt like a flashback to my younger days traveling in the Soviet Union with some Greek friends, where everyone was speaking English, but in accents I couldn't understand. "The gas station," my driver said, "where the taxis get their gas. I know where it is." But if taxi number one was in line with the cabs, I wondered, how was he at a gas station? It didn't make sense, but at this point, it was out of my hands.

As we pulled up to the gas station, my hopes fell. There was no cab visible. "He's not here," I said. "No," said the driver, "I don't see him."

And then, at the same moment, we both saw a slight, middle-aged man standing in the gas station parking lot, jumping up and down and waving his arms. It was our guy. He had left his cab in the line, somehow scaled a wire fence, and was waiting in the parking lot, waving my phone in his hands. He expressed his joy as freely as he had his frustration. I offered him a large reward, trying to put it into his hands, but he wouldn't take it. I hugged him and kissed him on the cheek instead.

In a matter of seconds, I was in the other cab again, racing back to the airport in a heady state of triumph. I really can't overstate my ebullience. I was as proud of my resourcefulness in pulling this off as if I had led the troops to victory. I thanked my second cab driver profusely and gave him a big tip. His driving had been both exciting and essential.

The rest of the trip was uneventful: even the usual irritation of the TSA experience felt soothing in its routine. It was too early in the morning to drink—although I was tempted—so I consoled myself with a latte and some $20 airport avocado toast. Still, I was reminded once again of the importance of kindness. One way or another, it will always come back to you.

It was a good day.

Tapestry

Over the course of the nearly twenty years we have lived here, there is a park with a particular route I have taken often with the dogs, through the woods and around an open field. It used to be an uncivilized, practically forgotten place where we never met anyone except skunks (with predictable results, see previous books), raccoons, and the occasional squirrel with a death wish. But sadly, the woods have been upgraded with wood-chipped paths, new signs announcing rules forbidding unleashed dogs, and other niceties that are not improvements. There are always people there, now, so we don't go very often anymore. There aren't many places where big dogs can just run free without other dogs around, so I feel very much that something has been lost.

When we do go, I choose odd times of day and bad weather, hoping to improve the odds that we won't encounter anyone so we can flout the rules with wildly happy, romping dogs. There are a few other stalwarts who seem to take the same approach.

One regular is a runner whom we have met on multiple occasions. He is not a young man. He has a long, grizzled beard, twinkly blue eyes, and a deeply genial and sincere manner. He drives a beat-up old pickup truck, which I have come to know. There is a place on the trail where people coming from opposite directions can suddenly encounter one another without warning, and the first time we met, it was there. The dogs were happily rummaging and trotting ahead of me when suddenly, there was a figure running toward us.

Immediately, I called Moses, the big, scary one, to my side, and he obeyed. But Pete, who is deaf, and Auggie, the headstrong puppy, would not come. Auggie throws himself at life in general, but also at turkeys, deer, strangers, and me in particular. I once looked out into the woods and saw Auggie joyously flying first at one line of turkeys—all four feet in the air—and, without waiting to see their startled flight into the trees, turning to hurl himself at the other line behind him. There is no malice in it, just pure exuberance, and even after two levels of obedience, it's a personality trait that I am having the devil of a time training out of him.

At nine months, Auggie is already well over ninety pounds, and once launched, he is a projectile who can take a person down. Now—to my horror—in his customary expression of puppy enthusiasm, Auggie ran to the man and joyously flung himself at his chest, paws first. I was expecting threats and anger, but instead the man laughed gently. "Hello, puppy!" he said, and kept running to the sound of my increasingly urgent commands mixed with profuse apologies. "It's okay," said the man as he ran past. "I like dogs."

Since then, we have met several times a month. Never at the same time. I take care now to take a different route so we can't accidentally encounter anyone. When I see the runner,

I call the big dogs and keep them off the path until he passes. He thanks me each time.

On Christmas Eve, on one of our solitary walks, we met him again. There was a little bit of fresh snow on the ground, and the dogs were filled with energy and eager to run. We went off on our different paths, and all was well. We were almost back to the car when I heard myself being called. The runner was coming toward me with his hand extended. "You dropped one of your leashes back there." I thanked him, surprised that he had come all the way back, out of his way, to do this nice thing.

The logistics would have been tricky, and it would probably have been a little odd, but I would like to have given him a Christmas present. He's a fairly random stranger, but I feel as if our encounters are important. Life's texture comes from these small things.

Looking Back;
Moving Forward

I have a big birthday coming up. It's one that forces me to take stock, to try to keep up with my own image of myself. I remember how my mother, when she was in her nineties, once sighed and said: "Oh, to be fifty-three again." It made me laugh at the time, but it helps me remember to appreciate life as it is now rather than worry about being older. I think the most successful—by which I mean happiest and most vibrant—older people are not those who dwell on numbers, or who talk about how old they are. Just as everyone always says, I still feel exactly the same inside as I did when I was a child, and I am determined to focus on living life, not on being a certain age.

For my last big birthday, my goals—started a few years in advance—were to write a book and to lose weight. I've published five books now, which I find somewhat surprising, but I haven't lost the weight. Or rather, I've lost it several times, but it keeps coming back with a vengeance. Maybe this decade.

I've lost people I loved in these past ten years. But I've also acquired some lovely new ones. There are new spouses and soon-to-be-spouses, and there are three new members of the next generation, with two more expected very soon. Altogether, the total number of new people is larger than the number lost. But still, there is an accumulation of sadness that comes from those losses, and it takes more and more effort to keep it at bay.

The total number of dogs is larger, too. We have gone from having two dogs to three. In this time, I was blessed with my very first German Shepherd. His short life didn't even span the decade. I used to think that when I got old, I would get smaller dogs, but now I doubt I'll ever have anything but a German Shepherd. Auggie will be four this year, and he has matured into a lovely, loyal, sensitive, and affectionate dog. Big baby Eli will turn one this month. It will be fun to see how he turns out, but for now, he is still a big old Rumbly-Bumbly, and very much the baby of the family.

I have two friends in their nineties. They are twins, and one was my mother's best friend. They have sent me two bottles of French champagne (is there any other kind?) for my birthday, and I am delighted by this expression of their world view and, perhaps, glimpse into their secret of longevity. I must have sent a somewhat plaintive letter, because one of them sent me a long and eloquent response about all the things she experienced in the thirty years between sixty and ninety. It was impressive, and inspiring, and beautiful.

I look in the mirror, and I see the changes of age, but I am still, essentially, myself, recognizable to someone who hadn't seen me in twenty years. And I am fortunate that my life's work isn't something I will have to age out of so long as my mind is still working. Sometimes I am tired, but I believe that is part of the pandemic: this somnolent, fairy-tale seclusion that seems so peaceful and without urgency.

And so, I look forward to the next phase of my life with hope and joy, ready for new adventures, grateful for my many blessings, and knowing that there are no guarantees.

Time to watch the sunrise.

❖ Moses

There comes a moment in grief when you begin to feel that you are being judged for it. People tell you that life goes on, that you need to stop looking back. I know that because, although I would never say it to anyone, I have often felt impatient with people who get into their problems and lie down in them. I have wanted to tell someone to get over it. In my own life, after various hard blows, including some difficult losses, I have managed to accept, to pick up the pieces of my life, and to move on. But it's closing in on two years later, and I still have not gotten over Moses.

Life has a way of teaching us our faults.

His full name was Moses, Prince of Egypt. My husband and I argued about the name all the way to Iowa when we went to pick him up for the first time. I was insistent. It had to be Moses. It wasn't a particularly religious choice. I had just watched too many reruns of *The Ten Commandments* and wanted to be able to shake my head sadly at a naughty puppy and say, "Oh, Moses, Moses, Moses."

The name suited him. Despite having been bitten by one as a child, I had wanted a German Shepherd my whole life. I had even made a German Shepherd a character in my novels. Readers who met Moses always assumed that my character

Elisabeth's big dog, Rocco, was based on him. But Rocco was really an expression of longing. He came first. Then came Moses. Sometimes I have the sense that I willed him into being.

And he did, after all, lead us out of the wilderness. Our beloved Golden Retriever had died after a futile battle with lymphoma. Our other dog, Pete, was grieving, and our house felt empty, so we decided to sign up for the twelve to eighteen month waiting list for the perfect German Shepherd. Within twenty minutes, we heard back. There had been a cancellation. Did we want a puppy on Saturday? I had the sense that it was meant to be, unplanned, the result of a series of unforeseeable events. And isn't that what Fate is? The inevitable coming together of paths that seemed intended to diverge? Does it always have to be a human story?

From the beginning, I knew he would break my heart. I loved him too much. I can't even explain exactly why. All I know is that there was a kind of destiny, an inevitability about him that I always felt. We belonged to each other. He was my soulmate. How to convey how much I loved him? How much I love him still? I know most people won't think it normal. I can't help that. It just was. It just is.

When he was only a few months old, I sat in our living room, holding him on my lap, hugging him and whispering endearments. He was already too big to really fit, but I had my arms around him like a baby. My husband walked into the room and said casually: "You love that dog too much. You know he's going to break your heart someday." To the surprise of us both, I burst into wild sobs.

I was afraid of him at first. I'd never had a German

Shepherd before, and I didn't have confidence in how to handle him. By the time he came along, I'd trained four dogs and felt that I knew what I was doing. But when he chewed a shoe and I slapped the floor with it, scolding to show my displeasure, he avoided that spot in the kitchen for three days. That's when I realized how delicate his sensibilities were. If I hurt his feelings, I could lose him forever.

But the moment that really frightened me was when, at nine weeks, I tried to pull him off the bed he had no permission to be on. He growled and snarled at me, and I was struck with fear that I had a dragon in the house that I could not control. I called my dog trainer that day and begged her to let us start early. He earned his first obedience title at six months, and his second not long afterward. It required retrieval, and he did not really take to retrieving, but he obliged me because that was what he did.

This is not to say that he was a tamed creature, tied to my will. Quite the contrary. Moses did things because he knew he should, and when I asked him to do something that was wrong for both of us, he would flat out refuse. One night, in the dead of a Wisconsin winter, I had an emergency call about my elderly mother. It was well below zero, and I had to meet the ambulance at the hospital. Moses knew I was upset, and he saw his job as being with me no matter what. But of course, he couldn't sit outside in the car for hours in sub-zero temperatures. He followed me out to the car, refusing to let me leave without him and trying to climb onto my lap. My husband gently put his hand on Moses's collar to pull him away, and Moses turned and very meaningfully put his teeth on my husband's arm. He did not bite; he nevertheless expressed his feelings very clearly. Moses knew his duty, and he was not easily dissuaded from it. I had to drive away from him, knowing we both felt betrayed by the separation.

I felt so much pride having this magnificent animal walk beside me. Moses loved going to the Fourth of July parade. The parade begins every year with a long line of historic fire engines, followed by the latest and most innovative as the proud company of volunteer firefighters marches along. Moses would sing with the fire engines, a long, lovely howl that made people turn and smile. He would sit upright and bark at the three-gun signal that began the parade, and he would duly accept the admiration of anyone who stopped to see him. When the parade was over, we would walk with the crowds down the street toward the park, and people would reach out their hands to touch him as he walked by, like Aslan at the resurrection.

There was a fierceness about Moses that is not in my other dogs. It lay beneath the surface, but it was right here for anyone to see. People respected Moses. As he deserved.

While we were remodeling our house, a five-man insulation team arrived one morning without notice. My husband and I were at work, and only the carpenter, who adored Moses, was there. The insulators opened the door and walked in. According to the carpenter, who laughed while telling the story, Moses chased all five of them "screaming like girls" into the powder room, where they all crowded in, slamming the door behind them.

They called their manager while Moses waited outside the door.

Moses had a passion for butter. When he was young, he would steal whole sticks of it from the plate on a high shelf next to the stove. After we broke that habit, he sang for his butter, his paws dancing as he looked from the butter dish to my face and back, carefully explaining what he wanted.

More than anything else, Moses loved the lake. He was the first of our dogs brought up to swim, and he took to it immediately. But it wasn't swimming that was his passion; it was splashing. His jumps to catch the water we splashed at him were stupendous. He leapt out of the water like a mythical beast, and his yearning to splash was relentless. If I were lazy and lounging on the dock, he would swim around the edge to me and paddle his paws to splash me, hoping to start a game. If I ignored him, he would urge me with increasingly louder moans of protest and pleading, splashing harder. He was impossible to resist.

There's a Christina Perry song from a silly vampire movie that I used to sing to Moses. I remember the last time we were at the lake, a few months before he died. The music came on, and I whispered it to him, holding him in my arms, tears rolling down my face.

I've loved you for a thousand years.
I'll love you for a thousand more.

I see now that I knew at some level it would be the last time we splashed together. Somehow, some part of me knew he was dying.

He had been in pain from an injured back, and it was slowing him down. I took him for exams. I asked every medical professional we saw—and there were a few—to reassure me that he would be all right. He's not going to die, is he? He'll be okay, won't he? They all, with varying degrees of patience and curiosity, assured me. Why would I even think that? He was only seven years old. His back hurt. That was all.

But they were wrong. Somehow, in the deep connection Moses and I had with one another, I sensed that something was wrong, but it was nothing that showed up on any tests. It was just arthritis pain from a back injury, nothing more, I was told. Of course he didn't feel well if his back hurt. We did acupuncture, chiropractic, and laser therapy. I took him for swimming therapy. He had varying levels of pain meds.

But he didn't look right. His eyes were glassy. His fur seemed without luster. And all the while, the tumor was growing unseen, waiting to break his heart, and mine.

What hurts me most is that I wasn't there. We had slipped away for three precious days to spend Christmas with our new baby granddaughter. While we were away, Moses had an upset tummy, but, like so many German Shepherds, he often did. We used to joke about such a big scary dog having "princess tummy." We also live in the woods, and the dogs tend to eat things that require periodic doses of antibiotics.

He was sad when we left. He knew what suitcases meant. But we were unconcerned because he would be in his own home with his brothers and someone who cared for him. Over the course of our trip, I spoke with the dog sitter multiple times. She was kind and reassuring. He wasn't sick, but he was moping. He wasn't eating, but he was drinking a lot of water. I was more worried about reassuring her than I was about Moses. We'd dealt with these tummy troubles before. I called the vet and arranged to pick up some antibiotics on the way home from the airport. We didn't know he would already be there, cooling on a metal table.

Our dog sitter, never imagining we would go to the vet first, waited at our house, dreading our return. She didn't want to tell us on the phone.

The one obligation of a soulmate is to be present when you die. But I wasn't there. Instead, while we were in the air, Moses lay down next to our dog sitter, put his paw on her arm, looked into her eyes, and let out a long sigh. Then he died.

Grief is one thing that never dies. I know it sounds overly dramatic, but I will never forgive myself. People have tried to tell me that he knew he shouldn't die in front of me. I don't buy it. He felt abandoned. He didn't know where I was. I let him down. I, who sang love songs to him, who loved and trusted him, for whom he would have laid down his life, wasn't there when he needed me most, and he died not knowing whether I would ever come back.

Looking back on that last year, I almost did the best I could. I didn't miss his cues. The mistake I made was believing everyone—good people who didn't know him as I did—who told me he was okay. I should have trusted my own heart. He was telling me, and I didn't take his word for it.

I will be haunted by his loss forever. My only hope is that those insipid rainbow bridge poems are true, and that someday he will run to me, and I will be able kneel down, gather him into my arms, and whisper my love into those big fierce ears.

Oh, Moses.

Oh, Moses, Moses, Moses.

Cold Feet ✦

I've heard older people say it more than once: you get to a point in life where you appreciate nice socks. I am a barefoot person, myself. In the house, out of the house, and whenever possible, I prefer bare feet. I like the feel of cool stone and polished wood. I feel as if my feet need to breathe.

It drove my mother crazy when I was a child, and my parents were continually worried I would get something in my foot. I rarely did. And as a result of years of going shoeless, the soles of my feet are as heavy with callouses as can be imagined. They are not beautiful, but they are damn near impermeable. In the summer, I rarely wear shoes, and then only sandals. At home I am barefoot.

For some reason, though, I recently developed a kind of mania for socks, and I'm wondering whether it's a sign of old age.

Maybe it's the pandemic.

It started with the realization that the approximately ten pairs of socks I had were developing holes. I cannot extend my love of going barefoot to exercise, so I needed new socks for my workouts. Simple enough. When they arrived, however, I realized that the new, inexpensive socks I had purchased were thin and poorly made, and their lack of quality bothered me.

Maybe with better socks, I could run faster. So, I bought some padded athletic socks that cushioned my feet. They were very soft and cushy, and this gave me an idea. Maybe I'd never liked socks because I hadn't bought nice ones. Armed with this stunning insight and a shopping app that made impulse purchases far too easy, I began my quest for the perfect socks. What else is there to do in a pandemic?

I bought acrylic socks in pastel pinks and lavenders; I bought woolen socks in jaunty argyle patterns; I bought alpaca socks in beautiful rich colors. For Valentine's Day, I bought heart socks for all my friends. Each new package arrived like a gift, filled with plushy delight. My new socks were soft, fuzzy, warm, thick, and delicious. Unfortunately, when I wore them, none of my shoes fit.

What's more, despite my best efforts—which are marginal and as easily subject to distractions as I am—the stone floor in my kitchen, although it looks perfectly respectable, always has a thin layer of grime, which collects relentlessly in the little stone crevices, and which is instantly detectable by any pair of socks. It's like the white glove treatment, but with feet.

The grime is a fringe benefit of loving three big dogs who also live with us in the woods, and whose paws, when they run, dig into the ground like mining equipment. I know from sad experience that completely eliminating the grime from the floor would be a task for a team of servants with scrub brushes, working more or less around the clock. A luxurious pair of beautiful, soft, pink alpaca socks would become a dingy gray in mere hours. Moments, even. So, I don't wear my socks while walking around. I do enjoy putting them on with my pajamas and walking briefly around the bedroom, however.

Then I read an article claiming that wearing socks to bed enhances sleep. The theory is that warm feet enhance vasodilation so that the blood can flow more easily, and the body core can cool more effectively in preparation for sleep. A confirmed insomniac, I thought this might be the perfect use for my new luxury socks. I tried it. For about five minutes. I couldn't stand it. Nice socks are nice socks, but for true comfort, bare feet must be permitted to dangle outside the covers in the cold.

So, my dresser drawer now bulges with socks of all colors, yarns, and purposes. I have socks for workouts, socks for after a warm bath, socks to match silk pajamas, socks to match old sweatshirts. I have plushy socks, warm socks, and insanely soft and delicate socks that feel like walking on marshmallows. Aside from the athletic socks, however, all are too thick to wear with shoes. And none are for walking in the kitchen.

I never wear them, but I do enjoy opening the drawer and looking at them. I suppose that according to my own youthful frame of reference, I am now, technically, an old person. But I will have to eschew the socks.

❖ Electronic Narcissism

I like silence. Perhaps it is a commentary on the state of my nerves, or maybe it's because I'm a former musician and my brain is aurally focused, but I find unwanted noises distracting. I need silence to think and to write, and when I want sound, I prefer to choose whether it's words or music. So, I find the contemporary taste for household appliances that ping, beep, and play tunes extremely annoying.

If I seem cranky, it's probably because I have been trying desperately to write a novel amidst continual interruption from household appliances. I have a notion that devices should a) make your life easier and b) not require distraction from your thoughts and, come to think of it, c) achieve their purposes in silence while leaving me alone.

In my quest to break my writing stalemate, I recently packed up and left home for the seclusion of the Island. The house I rent when I go away to write is a place I know well. I have been going there for years, and it's like a second home. It's a charming place, roomy, but cozy, with a wonderful property where I can walk in privacy with the dogs, and a lovely landlady who knows the precise formula of solitude and companionship to feed a writer. I have written parts of all my books there, and there's something about the atmosphere that inspires productivity. My days there are a perfect pattern of writing and walking, and no one disturbs me unless I want to be disturbed. The house is not old, but my landlady had just replaced the range, the refrigerator, and the washer-dryer, all sparkling new and ready to be used. She is a generous woman and likes to buy quality things.

Throughout my first day, unfortunately, I spent a great deal of time debating when to tell my host that there were red squirrels nesting in the roof. I knew it would upset her, and I also knew it would mean workmen disrupting my writing. The squirrels' chirping and scratching was irregular but loud, and I feared they were doing damage. It wasn't until late in the afternoon that I finally realized that it wasn't squirrels, but the new refrigerator. I have no idea why a refrigerator should make a noise like red squirrels. Maybe someone thought it was cute. Or maybe no one ever spent any time in a room where it was running. I suppose it was companionable, in its way. I mean, at least the noise resembled living things.

The stove however, was much worse than squirrels. Writing can be both lonely and vaguely excruciating, and it is during these moments that I usually take a break to cook something nice for myself. Sometimes the food in my novels is actually something I've just made. Food, for me, is comfort, and when I'm alone, I look forward to meals as a way of permitting myself a break and as a kind of companionship. In some ways, it's as much about the cooking as it is about the eating. Cooking is a pleasant diversion, and creative, but as I'm chopping onions or browning beef, my mind is able to continue the intellectual rambling necessary for building a story.

So, having grown accustomed to the refrigerator squirrels, after a few hours of work and a long walk in lovely silence, I turned on the oven, and was jolted out of my plot-related reverie by a jaunty little tune. It wasn't just a beep but an actual musical phrase, only with tinky-tonk noises. When I set the timer, it produced another tune, and like so many electronic devices, instead of one smooth dialing motion to set the temperature, I had to press it each time I added ten degrees, each time producing another beep. When the oven reached the temperature I had laboriously set, it sang yet another tune. Apparently, each melody has a specified meaning, but I'm not interested in providing room in my head for determining which is which. I found myself missing my vintage stove at home, whose only noise is the satisfying "whomp" it makes when you light the oven with a match.

Then there was the new washing machine. I pack lightly when I go away to write. I mean to say, the car is full of stuff— much of it dog-related, and some of it bourbon—but I don't bring a lot of clothes, so I'm happy to have a washer-dryer in the house, and I often throw something into the washer while I'm writing. This new machine could be featured in a museum as The Loudest Washing Machine in the World, and it makes what I can only describe as a rhythmic mechanical gagging sound for the entire cycle. It's some sort of water-saving design, which is, I guess, mandatory, but seems a little silly when you're only steps away from—literally—a quadrillion gallons of water. I found the gagging somewhat less charming than the nesting squirrels. As if this were not enough, it beeps. Not once, for each time you choose a cycle, or once when it's finished, but every 30 seconds after the cycle until you interrupt the sentence you're writing to get up and open the lid. I have had the care of less demanding puppies.

Thankfully, I was able to close the door to drown out the worst of the noises, but the beeping penetrated the walls. Not surprisingly, the matching dryer is also an electronic nag. But the thing is, if they make weird gurgling noises and show signs of nausea, how would you know until you got them home? I have a new washer and dryer at home, and they both have the options to turn off the signals. I made sure of that. Of course, I don't live in the same room with them, either. So, there's that.

But still.

It used to be that appliances would sit silently and make themselves useful. Now, for reasons I do not understand, they seem to feel a need to call attention to themselves, as if, like electronic toddlers, they are announcing: Look at me! Look what I've done!

A friend of mine was in an appliance showroom recently when a strange man sidled up to her. "Don't get that one," he said, *sotto voce*. "It's got wi-fi. My kids run loads, forget about them, and leave the house. The damned thing keeps calling me at the office until someone opens the lid."

It all strikes me as an indication of a deeply flawed society. What personal failings have led us to develop narcissistic appliances? Is it a reflection of modern life, the electronic equivalent of so-called influencers, who must announce their doings on Twitter, Instagram, Pinterest, and Facebook or be forced to question the value of their own existences? Have we created appliances like ourselves? Is there anyone who likes this incessant mechanistic signaling? Or is there something about the electronic miasma in which we all exist that assimilates our nerves into a state of noise acquiescence? Is there some consumer movement I need to join to dissuade manufacturers from this evil path?

The last time I bought a microwave oven, I asked the saleswoman which ones beeped only once and stopped. It was clear by her reaction that no one else had ever asked this question, but she dutifully investigated the beeping of each one, no doubt thinking words that I am grateful not to have heard. But each time I buy a new appliance, I find that the noise factor has intensified as if this has become a signal—as it were—of improvement. I believe it is, instead, an instrument of consumer torture.

A few days after I got home and settled into a new appreciation of my quiet appliances, the brand new, very expensive water heater silently burst a valve and unobtrusively leaked water all over the basement floor.

I felt oddly grateful.

Seeds ✤

We have a big yard and lots of dogs. There are advantages to having a big yard for the dogs. But if you have a yard, you tend to have weeds. And if you have dogs, you probably shouldn't use weed killers. My scientist father, who loved nature, raised me with a healthy skepticism of poisons for weeds and poisons for creatures. But I am a gardener. This is why I have been engaged in a protracted battle with dandelions for some years. The dandelions are winning.

For me, the sight of those puffy seed heads, which, as children we used to blow away with a puff of breath as we sat idly in the shade of our parents' lawns, are an abomination. They foretell the growth of new dandelions, stubbornly concealed among the foliage of my garden beds until they burst into bloom, their long, carroty roots embedded in the earth, their removal requiring much disruption of my established plants. I don't actually care if they're in the grass, which may be the root—as it were—of my problem.

My husband works from home, and when we're at our tiny lake cottage, for the hour or so he's recording a podcast, the dogs and I need to be outside or hiding in a bedroom upstairs. Today was beautiful, so we went outside to sit and doze in the sun. It's permission to do nothing, and we all enjoy it.

As I sat idly, I saw a seed head in the sun, and it suddenly struck me how beautiful it was. The sphere comprised of perfectly formed little flying machines, designed to populate the world with yellow flowers for wine and long, edible, carroty roots and leaves for salads. Dandelions are delicious, I guess, but I only remember the bitter taste on my fingers after picking them. I've never made wine from them, but the romance of it has resonated with me since I first started reading Ray Bradbury in my adolescence.

How is it that we've come to dislike such beautiful yellow flowers that grow with no effort on our part? That send seeds dancing on the wind through some remarkable engineering? That feed bees, and help them make honey, and nourish us, and give us wine to make us happy, and basically take care of themselves?

Remind me again why I have grass.

Burial at Sea ✳

A dark red sun rises in a lavender sky colored by smoke from fires more than a thousand miles away. A juvenile owl makes intermittent pulsating squawks from deep in the woods until the light comes, or until it is fed. The itinerant geese, who have restless nights, have been stirring for some time. The sunlight has begun to penetrate the woods in pink shafts. I can see the shadows of creatures moving through the backlit brush. Maybe deer. Maybe coyote. Maybe turkey. A big hawk perches on a precarious branch.

All the world reveals itself in morning as it has for millennia and will for millennia more. But Margaret is not here.

I got a call yesterday morning, and when I saw the name, I guessed what the news would be. She would have been 90 on October 6th, my godmother and friend, an inveterate dog lover. She called me "lovey." No one else will do that now.

It seems strange that so deep a change should go unnoticed in the universe. It strikes me anew each time someone I care about dies. It feels to me as if it were a burial at sea, where the one you love dips beneath the waves of time and disappears forever.

Farewell Margaret Rose. You were beloved.

✤ The Roots of Faith

I have lost the thread of my conversations with God. I know that this sense of losing contact is common among even the most ardent believers along with periods of doubt and complete lapses of faith, but knowing it doesn't reassure me.

We have had high winds this past twenty-four hours, and two big trees went down along our path through the woods. It is still windy this morning and bitterly cold, and I am listening for the sound of another tree going down. The dogs are edgy, restless, and I don't want them out for long for fear their ramblings in the woods might take them to the wrong place at the wrong moment when a big branch comes hurtling to the ground.

But sometimes it's when the wind stops that the greatest danger comes. That's often the time when the great old trees let go—those hollowed by time or insects or weakened by water. Slowly, there comes a deep stirring in the earth, a heavy rustling of leaves that resonates oddly as a warning, and then the boom, as the house shakes, and the windows, and the tree gives way to the ground.

Here, in our woods, there are too many fallen trees to keep up with, and so the fallen lie as memorials to the past. I dream of hiring teams of woodcutters to collect them all and take the wood away. There's more than we could burn in a dozen lifetimes, and there are still plenty of hollow trees and stumps and piles to make homes for all the creatures who wish to stay.

The fallen trees feel important in a way I cannot name, but which I think is related to my estrangement from God. Science has convinced me that my childhood belief in the souls of trees is true. Mock me if you like, but for many years, scientists accused us of anthropomorphizing animals, only to belatedly discover that they have thoughts and feelings, all signs—I believe—of souls. So, I feel justified in my conviction that trees have souls, too. Perhaps it's my Celtic ancestry. I am sure, in any case, that they are living creatures who deserve, at the very least, respect, if not reverence. Each is an irreplaceable, once-in-all-eternity individual with, as science has now learned, connections to their communities, respect for other individuals, and nurture of one another with signals, and instructions, and advice for survival.

Trees are not animals, but they, too, live, and in an era when the warming earth concerns us, the contribution of trees to the protection of the atmosphere continues to be undervalued. We should be alarmed when they sicken and plant more before they fall. A fine tree should be treasured by the community, not ripped out to widen roads.

My own small town recently ripped out a long hedge of lilacs to make a turning lane for the post office on a minor rural road that has no significant traffic. The hedge—probably seventy years old—had been at least twenty feet high and fifty feet long, and its purple fragrance wafted into car windows

Building Jerusalem

Yesterday I took a handful of earth and sprinkled it over Margaret's grave. It's a ritual whose insight was born in millennia of human grief, giving hard reality to the shock and disbelief of those first days, and forcing confrontation with the black hole of mourning. It was a pandemic service—small and outdoors, with only fourteen of us—and in the midst of wild autumn storms, the rain stopped, and from a deep blue sky, the sun shone on the yellow leaves above my home church's tiny columbarium.

Margaret and I spent time together last week for only the second time since the pandemic. I brought Eli to visit, and we went for a walk. She gave Eli treats. Her daughter texted me that night to say that Margaret was the happiest she had been in a long time; how excited she was about Eli; how beautiful she had found him. I examined my conscience about why I had not gone to see her sooner, but I am still desperately grateful that we had that afternoon.

Margaret Rose was born in Sheffield England in 1930, a contemporary of the princess who shared her name. Sheffield was a manufacturing town, and when the blitz came, it was heavily targeted by the Nazis. She lived with her family in a block of rowhouses, all sharing a wall with the house next door.

When the air raids came, the neighbors would crawl through holes in the cellar walls to huddle together, perhaps trying to get the little ones to sleep.

One morning they emerged from their shelter after a night of bombing and found that the other side of the street—identical to their own—had been flattened. Everyone was dead.

Her father packed them up and walked the three miles to the bus stop so they could stay with an aunt in the country. As they passed through the devastated city, he hoisted Margaret's little sister onto his shoulders and told his children to close their eyes so as not to see the gruesome sights of human carnage along the way. "Close your eyes and take my hand. Trust me." Margaret peeked, and to the end of her life she was haunted by the sights of her neighbors' arms and legs lying disconnected among the rubble.

She told me she still dreamed of the terror of those nights, the bombs screaming and exploding, the children crying, the adults bravely cheerful in the face of utterly random death. From the safety of her aunt's house, they watched as the night sky above Sheffield—some thirty miles away—lit up with fire. Sheffield was bombed nearly to obliteration, and the casualties were overwhelming.

Life was unimaginably hard. The rubble from the bombings wasn't cleared away because there was no one to clear it: all the men were at war.

There was a shortage of everything: housing, clothing, fuel, and food. Margaret had a passion for chocolate that may have intensified in the rationing of sugar, butter, flour, milk, eggs, meat, and chocolate. Her mother and father would give her their chocolate ration cards, knowing how much she adored it.

Margaret had a collection of stories, and she told them regularly. She was, in Ray Bradbury's interesting observation, a living time machine, able to bring to life moments that to me seemed ancient history. As she approached her ninetieth birthday, her short-term memory was failing dramatically, but she remembered the past in great detail. Her conversation was sprinkled with her well-worn tales, told anew as to a fresh audience. Each visit, each phone conversation became a ritual of story and repetition, a bit like the comforting ritual of the Anglican Church to which we both belong. At first, I was frustrated and inwardly impatient, but she took the same pleasure in telling each time, so I learned to lean back and allow her stories to wash over me, giving her the responses I thought she would like most, even if I'd heard it again only a few moments before.

She married the love of her life, a British airman, and together they emigrated to Canada, and then to the United States. They loved to dance. They participated in theater. They had a family with children and grandchildren and many dogs.

Margaret was a dog lover from her earliest days. She worked as a volunteer at the local Humane Society for years, and inevitably brought more than one home. "I couldn't live without dogs," she told me. Her mother had forbidden dogs in the house, and one of Margaret's stories told how her father had brought home a collie puppy one day, and her mother had made him take it back. "I hated her for that!" Margaret would say with delight at her own naughtiness. As soon as she had her own house, she was never without a dog again.

After her husband died, we went to church together now and then when she could no longer drive. It was good to go home to the church and sit in the pews with old friends. Sometimes it was sad to look around and see the congregation diminishing, favorite faces gone forever.

At the funeral, I sang *Jerusalem*, that paean to British faith and spirit. It was outside, without the organ, so I stood on the steps leading down into the little brick-pathed columbarium, facing the small cluster of people, my eyes on the trees above them so I didn't have to see their reactions. It's difficult to sing at funerals at the best of times, but singing for someone you care about is hard. I made it almost to the end before my voice caught on the last four words. In that split second, I saw the priest's eyes turn to me in alarm before I gathered myself to finish.

As I drove home, I took a wandering back roads route, revisiting the countryside where I grew up, past the farms of old school friends' families, past the little waysides I remembered. Here was where my friend and I stopped on our bikes one hot day, here's where my best friend's grandparents lived, here's where the school bus stopped when I came home with her. There's the stone farmhouse I used to dream of owning. The sky was filled with storm clouds and sunshine.

As I rambled around the narrow back roads, a flash of white caught my eye. There was a bald eagle perched on a dead tree, huge and proud. Her mate was circling overhead, perhaps enjoying the currents from the storms. I thought of Margaret's love of nature, and her oft-repeated story of her father's Sunday lectures on trees, and I remembered the words of the hymn.

Bring me my bow of burning gold,
Bring me my arrows of desire.
Bring me my spear. O, clouds unfold!
Bring me my chariots of fire.
I will not cease in mental fight,
Nor shall my sword sleep in my hand,
'Til we have built Jerusalem
in England's green and pleasant land.

I thought of Margaret's stories. The love, the terror, the rebuilding, the long walks. The angers and the joys, the frustrations and the consolations. I knew so many of the high and the low points because she had built the stories for me, unintentionally ensuring I remembered through their repetition.

She often told me how fortunate she was to still live on her own in a pleasant place surrounded by paths, trees, gardens, and a lake where she walked daily. Her death came suddenly, without lingering, at a healthy old age. It is the best any of us can hope for. And, then I remembered the last line of my favorite Willa Cather story, and a wave of peace washed over me.

Margaret's life seemed to me complete and beautiful.

❧ Signs of Hope

I was watching a small drama this morning at dawn. The polar vortex has moved on, the -22 temperatures have risen more than forty degrees, and the vicious winds, creating a wind chill factor of forty or fifty below zero, have died. I have been worried about the wild animals, knowing that this weather kills many birds and probably mammals, too. I have not seen a single squirrel in a week, and this is highly irregular. The turkeys, normally restless and predictable in their daily patterns, have not followed their usual path but stayed beneath the trees where they roost, puffed into enormous balls of feather, clustered together like giant mushrooms.

I put out seed, and fruit, and all kinds of nuts, suet balls with nuts and meal worms, and big chunks of suet in fat strips from the butcher, which I have to shoo the dogs from. The fat has drawn crows, whom I rarely see up close, and that makes me happy. We have springs on our property, so we don't have to worry about a water supply, but still, this is a hard season for creatures. Many times over the past week, I thought of the animals, curled up, trying to keep warm in their trees or burrows, and I felt helpless pity.

This morning, though, as I was watching the sunrise, I noticed a black mass against the side of a tree deep in the woods. Suspicious, I watched until I saw it move. It was a raccoon, returning home from its nighttime ramble. And then I saw a second raccoon, climbing up the same trunk in a congenial fashion. So, this is how they survive the cold. I was enchanted. A pair! There will be babies!

As I watched their clumsy, though expert climb, I was cheered by the thought of their snuggling together in the winter weather. And then I peered more closely. Not two. Three raccoons. Clearly joining forces to keep one another warm. Were they siblings? In this woods, probably. They were all fat, but not as big as some I've seen, possibly yearlings. They each perched on a separate branch, far more precariously than any turkey. Turkeys, after all, can fly. And although there was one spectacular slip and fall to a lower branch, the raccoons all managed to stay on the tree without falling fifty feet to the ground.

I wonder whether this arrangement is long-term or merely expedient, but the sight of this little pack, or family, or club, delighted and distracted me. I watched, my coffee growing cold, as they settled in uncomfortable-looking poses on their separate, too-small branches until they each made their way back to the trunk where they had their beds and disappeared, presumably until night falls again, when they can resume their sociable adventurings.

All is well.

Pandemic Squalor

Every morning, I've been taking a bath with a spider. I know what you're thinking, and honestly, I'm not a spider fan myself. But I discovered him the other day as I was filling the tub, and he was so small and vulnerable, I felt protective. I used a subscription card from a shelter magazine and urged him to climb aboard before he could be scorched or drowned.

I imagine he lives in one of the orchids that sit sulking around the edge of the tub. I remember to water them sometimes—usually with bath water slightly cooled—and this seems to be a good plan for orchids, because once a year or so, one of them ceases its lackluster loitering and bursts into bloom while the rest hang their heads and look vaguely ratty. In the spring, I gather them up, reserving for myself whichever one is most likely to produce flowers soon, and hand them over to the lovely man who tidies my flower garden to give to his orchid-loving wife for restoration. Last time he protested that she had told him if he brought home one more orchid, she would serve it to him on a plate. (Are orchids poisonous?) So, I fear this avenue may be lost to me, and I will now either have to allow the collection to linger—flourishing seems beyond us both—or stop buying orchids altogether, even though they are so tempting in the hardware store, all beautifully encased in bloom and bud, and not sulky at all.

In any case, since that first morning, the spider has been joining me in the bath, and we have come to an understanding that if he stays away from the place I put my head, I will keep the water level low enough not to disturb him. I watch for him every morning and once had to fish him out with the handmade, wooden, Ukrainian sauna ladle I bought online in a fit of something or other. I hadn't realized it would come shipped directly from the craftsman in Ukraine—nor that it would be roughly the size of a tennis racquet—so I was somewhat nonplussed when, in the early days of the pandemic with paranoia at its pinnacle, an enormous package arrived in the mail with Cyrillic writing and odd stamps. I couldn't for the life of me imagine who was sending me packages from Ukraine, and was it a death threat, or possibly anthrax, and I left it sitting on the wooden bench outside the door for three days while I tried to figure it out.

I realize that I am giving the impression of somewhat lackadaisical and disordered housekeeping—if not actual insanity—what with the spiders, the sullen orchids, and mysterious packages lying about outdoors, to say nothing of the dog hair, the mud, and the utterly uncontrollable stacks of mail—most of it not quite important, but almost important, and which therefore must be opened and then shredded or burned rather than merely thrown away, and dealing with it requires a certain amount of will for the surmounting of tedium. There are also piles of laundry—mostly clean—which neither my husband nor I enjoy putting away.

It wasn't always this way. My house had, until now, been beautiful, impeccable … curated even. But the pandemic—and my reluctance to bring outsiders into the house, unvaccinated as so many people seem to be—has forced me to face the domestic routine by myself, half-heartedly and with tiny bursts of energy to attack it, then running out of interest and forced by ennui to look away. There are dog hair dust bunnies in the corners that I never seem able to eliminate, dust accumulates everywhere at a rate with which my air purifiers are unable to cope, there are spider webs sprawling inside the storm windows, and the mild winter means mud, and muddy dog feet, and my several mopping and vacuuming robots are not quite equal to the task. As a result, the house has acquired a seedy, unkempt feeling which depresses me.

But the spider, despite his being squalor-adjacent, for some reason cheers me, and I am perfectly happy to share my baths with him so long as he shows no inclination to bring along any larger friends. These are the kinds of things the pandemic has brought me to.

Oh well. We carry on.

The World as We Once Knew It

When I'm walking the island, my mind wanders to many things. Sometimes they're related to the book—I often work through plot ideas while I'm walking—but not always. I have learned through hard experience that if I don't record the idea, it will disappear forever. In fact, if my notes are too cryptic, they may still be unfathomable. Yesterday I had a thought about the corona virus and the Greek gods. I don't know why. They were trapped in quarantine on Olympus and bickering together—it made me laugh. But there was another idea—what was it?

Maybe not so funny is the fact that quarantine's illusion of immortality—of time stretching on infinitely—took away that sense we ought to have of racing against a waning lifetime. Maybe it was a respite for a while. Maybe it was a relief not to have to keep churning. But that idleness—that missing sense of time passing—is precisely what made the gods so mischievous. They had no real purpose, no goals. They were, in a word, bored. And aimless. Okay, two words.

But for mortals, it was an illusion. Time does pass. As survivors, we are, of course, just as old as we would have been otherwise. Or maybe, had the pandemic not happened, we would have been out in the world and hit by a bus. We can't know. What we do know is the great loss, if not of someone we knew and cared about, then of community, of ourselves, of the world as we once knew it, of our precious time on earth. I feel new sympathy for the unjustly imprisoned, who must have some version of this same feeling: the sense of having been robbed of time. But especially for those whose lives were so directly affected by the illness itself.

But as with all forms of grief, we must choose either to lie down in it and never look up or to get up and get on with things, knowing that, whether we choose it or not, some new grief or old will be waiting to pop out at us when we are unwary.

We move onward, with resignation and hope together. To do otherwise is to die too soon.

Sunrise Monotony ✤

Mid-pandemic, I no longer remember dates, and sometimes I don't recall on a Thursday what I did on Sunday. But I remember with odd specificity the sunrises I watch each morning from my big picture window. Our house sits on a ridge looking down at the valley of a trout-filled creek. At this time of year, with the leaves still off the trees, I can see the clouds of mist rising from Lake Michigan three miles away.

I rise early to write—with varying success these days—and drink my coffee in a big, comfortable swivel chair, a fire in the fireplace, a candle burning, and my various dogs strewn about in poses of restless anticipation.

Today I am determined to leave my cell phone with its social media temptations in another room, so I am not able to take my usual morning photo. But the trees seem outlined with a rare clarity, and the sky, just above the deep blue lake mists that sit along the horizon like a mountain range, is a brilliant pink. For the fourth or fifth time this winter, the snow is almost completely gone, and this time may be for good. It has been a disappointing winter with little snow, and I am not someone who rejoices in summer. Too many bugs.

I am fortunate to have the leisure to sit and watch the

sunrise. It wasn't always so. I remember standing at these windows, dressed for the office, wistfully watching the beginnings of dawn and wishing with all my power that I could stay at home, drinking coffee in the company of my dogs. On those rare days when I could stay home, I would say to the dogs: "Today we're going to have a happy, happy day!" Now I say it to remind myself of how lucky I am.

But watching the sunrises is now a part of every day. I rise in the dark, spurred on by the prickings of my conscience—what are you for if not to write? This is what your life is for. The restless stirrings of the dogs, who know the routine better than I, make sure I get up when I should.

Today, in the March transition from winter to spring and back again, the air is colder than the water, causing the mists from the lake, but the line of sky above them is now a translucent blue-green. I can see the silhouettes of turkeys roosting in the trees and the first peach warmth in the sky, much further sorth than a week ago. The dogs are asleep again, now satisfied that I will not be doing anything that interests them for some time, and I can hear their breathing in the dark.

In this almost monastic life I live now, the sunrises exist not as blur, but each with its own character—some brilliant, some subtle, some merely a change of light. They are a marking of the days, but I understand, too, that they are also a celebration of creation as powerful to me as any morning mass.

When the phone is in my hand, I look away. Now that I understand, I am leaving the phone behind, a challenge as daunting as abstention to an alcoholic. It's okay, though. Turns out I don't need photos to remember.

New Beginning ✤

We got the second vaccine. Having heard that there could be symptoms, I filled the kitchen with popsicles, ginger ale, bread, crackers, and grapes. I arranged for our friend to walk the dogs and made their dinners in advance. Afterward, we celebrated with a very rare trip to the best custard stand in the world and took a selfie together, holding our waffle cones in triumph. We went to bed almost giddy with delight.

We woke up in the middle of the night in misery: fever, chills, headache, nausea, and the feeling that we had been beaten all over.

The dogs, of course, in their inimitable fashion, decided to help. Pete, in a break from routine, felt that a midnight outing might be in order. Eli, sensing distress, climbed onto the bed to step on my hair and drop dirty socks—rescued from the hamper—on our faces. Auggie, desperately trying to protect me and blocked from getting close by big old Rumbly-Bumbly, as my husband calls the puppy, ended by growling terrifyingly in real anger and biting Eli on the nose, hard. Eli, quite naturally, peed on the comforter. The aching was so terrible that I could barely use my arms but removing the comforter from the bed became an instant prime directive. It fell next to Pete's bed, making him afraid to walk past it and leaving him to pace and cry piteously until I roused myself a second time and dragged it out of his way.

My husband, just as sick as I and blessed with the ability to sleep through anything, slept through everything.

By morning, we felt, if anything, worse. My husband roused himself to drink coffee and send off a newsletter. I focused my eyes on it long enough to proofread it, then put a pillow over my head and lay in a state of misery the rest of the day. I drank ginger ale and ate a few crackers but was otherwise unable to eat even toast.

I woke the next morning feeling somewhat battered but on the mend. By the end of the day, I felt completely back to normal. (But I had a weird headache for the rest of the week.)

We are so grateful. The end is the beginning of life again.

Detox ✦

The house we rented in Maine is very old and very large. It has history. Perched on a small hill above the lake, it has sprawling porches front and back and lovely views. There's a spacious kitchen, a laundry room, and five roomy bedrooms with four baths. There's a massive stone fireplace in the living room. But it does not have wi-fi, and the cell signal is only one elusive bar, which seems to flit from room to room like a butterfly and then disappear.

It has been a long time since I have left my phone sitting on the nightstand, turned off, and walked away for the day. I feel released from electronic bondage. The impulse, in an idle moment, to look down at the phone is gradually being replaced by a willingness to look up, to think, to let my brain idle. That's how writing happens.

I had become increasingly aware of the way my phone had taken over my life. I am continually scrolling through my messages. There's not a scene that passes before my eyes that doesn't make me reach for the camera. There's not a drive that isn't accompanied by a podcast.

It's too much. It's too many voices. It's too much externality. And none of those things are good for a writer.

This week I wrote in the mornings. I hung around with

my family. We worked on a complicated jigsaw puzzle. I sat on the dock and dangled my feet and thought about things. I jumped into the cold lake. I cuddled children. I drank cocktails. I went to bed with a book.

It was a kind of detox, and it has put me on the path to getting my brain back.

The temptations to return to my old habits will be strong, and I imagine there will be a gradual regression toward overuse. But I have a plan to keep it in check, and at the moment, it doesn't even seem appealing to go back to my old ways.

But addiction is hard. We'll see.

Condolence ✤

I remember the numbness after my father died. The grief. The relief. The worry about my mother, the lone survivor of their sixty-year relationship.

It was in the hours between midnight and dawn when I came home from the hospital and found my mother sitting in the kitchen, one light on, my father's big dog, Rudy, at her feet.

"Rudy woke me up," she said. "Before you called."

It had not been the loving vigil I had wanted. My brother had come from out of state to say goodbye while my father lived. My sister stayed at the house with my mother. I was alone at my father's bedside. His pain had been so terrible that day, we begged the nurses for more drugs. They may have dulled, but they did not soothe. His hallucinations then filled him with terror. "Don't kill me!" he cried out, as the nurses were gently tending him. Were his last thoughts only of fear? Was there any comfort remaining to him, or only nightmare?

When he went back under, I wanted to put my hand on his forehead, to kiss him, to hold his hand, to reassure him, but I was afraid of reawakening the terror. So, I did not touch him. I stayed near, as quietly as I could. It did not occur to me to try to sing to him, or to read to him. And even now, many years later, I'm still not sure whether he would have wanted that. Maybe it would have been an intrusion. I was afraid only of reawakening his heartbreaking fear. Surely quiet sleep was better. Soon, the silence and depth of the night overtook me, and I fell asleep on the couch near his bed. I'm sure he felt he'd died alone.

It was not a good death.

Pete's death was not a good death, either. After months of luring us into complacency about the imminence of his end, the crisis came suddenly. He, too, cried out in pain or fear, and we couldn't get to the emergency room fast enough; he was almost gone by the time we arrived. But he was in my husband's arms the whole time, hearing, I hope, the soft crooning Pete knew meant love. That's a bit better, maybe.

My father was a man who lived a life of decency, integrity, and honor. He was a genuinely good person. So were my mother, and my aunt, and my mother-in-law, all of whom died in some unique form of misery. I suspect the notion of a good death is pure illusion, and I doubt many of us are vouchsafed such a thing. But maybe Pete, in his infinite canine goodness, had earned something no human being—no matter how good—could ever hope for.

Sometimes I find comfort in that.

Family Conspiracy ✦

I believed in Santa Claus until I was almost ten.

It's not that I was a particularly stupid child, but my sister and brother were fourteen and eleven years older, so I had, essentially, four adults in the house conspiring against me. When I began to ask pointed questions, they always had an answer. The evidence provided to my eyes and ears was so convincing that I would present it to my skeptical friends with the calm certainty of a prosecuting attorney.

In the run-up to Christmas, there would be sleigh marks in the snow, cleverly provided by my sister's boyfriend on skis. If there were sounds on the roof from scampering squirrels, then it must have been Santa Claus. There were mysterious bells in the hallway at night. Later in the year, even the Easter bunny—clearly part of the Santa Claus mystique—would leave telltale bits of rabbit fur, which bore a curious resemblance to a dachshund's. My world was ringed with seasons of mystery and excitement, but my credulity must also have been a way of keeping the wonder alive for my world-weary teenaged siblings.

Christmas at our house was permeated in wondrous events. The tree, duly purchased by my parents and lit by my father, would be put up on Christmas Eve. It was always as high as the ceiling, and it had to be a balsam. When I went to bed, it was bare, but in the morning, it was sparkling with ornaments and tinsel because Santa himself had decorated it. This act of pure magic was so potent and beautiful that I still long for it in my dreams. My older brother, for as long as I believed, refused to take part in decorating so that he, too, could still be surprised, if not actually blessed with the mystery of the thing.

After the excitement of the presents, there would be time to go around the tree searching for my favorite ornaments. There were large silver and green globes of solid glass that had belonged to my German great-grandparents, and fragile, whisper-thin glass hot air balloons covered with netting from the same era, and gold and green balls with loose strands of beading around them that formed a sort of sling. There was a hot pink helicopter, that must have been purchased for my brother when he was little, and a small red demon creature with piercing eyes, which my father playfully named Ethel after my mother. The tree was covered in tinsel and rain, some of the tinsel so old that it was still made of metal.

In traditional fashion, I left cookies and milk for Santa and one turnip for the reindeer. The next morning, the cookies and milk were gone, and the remainder of the turnip would have delicate tooth marks, not so much like reindeer teeth. Every year I argued with my mother that one turnip was a stingy gift for eight—or possibly nine—reindeer, but she insisted that after eating turnips at so many children's houses, the reindeer wouldn't be all that hungry. I was never satisfied by this. Santa, after all, got a full plate of cookies, and the reindeer had all the work of flying. It wasn't until later that I learned that the job of leaving tooth marks in the turnip was contemplated with dread by all. I have a mental picture of my family drawing straws, with the loser reluctantly accepting the raw turnip and gnawing away while the others laughed and carried on with the less onerous job of decorating the tree. I presume the main part of the turnip was cut off and saved for Christmas dinner, with only the stem end left to chew, but I can't imagine why no one suggested I leave carrots or apples instead.

Santa always left a thank you note—manners were inculcated at every opportunity—in a beautiful swirling script befitting a man of magic and mystery but actually belonging to my artistic sister. (The Easter Bunny, who also left notes, wrote in block letters with an engineering pencil from my inventor father's desk. Bunnies should be proud of having any writing skills at all, without having to worry about aesthetics. Apparently, though, between the time when my siblings were believers and my arrival on the scene, Santa's writing miraculously changed from block letters to script.)

Santa's notes were perfunctory, but to hold a piece of paper that he had touched, and to see my name written in his hand was a thing more marvelous than the stacks of gifts around the tree. "Dear Janet," it would say. "Thank you for the cookies. The reindeer enjoyed their snack, too. Love, Santa." I imagine now there was a note of sarcasm in the remarks about the turnip.

My gifts were often intricate projects made in turns by the whole family. A trio of Barbie-sized Steiff bears had handmade green felt alpine vests and hats for the papa and the baby, a red striped apron for the mama, along with three home made beds—one too big, one too small, and one just right. Three different sized, roughly-made white wooden chairs were painted with "Papa," "Mama," and "Baby" across the backs. They matched a table whose top was cut from a slice of the parquet floors from the new addition that had made room for me. There was a handmade Mary Poppins doll whose yarn hair was fashioned neatly in a bun, with her own hand-embroidered carpet bag, and sets of clothes so perfectly made—complete with linings—I wish I had some of them for myself now; a felt set of the entire Babar family (Arthur was my favorite for some reason); beautifully sewn doll clothes; and handmade books with stories written just for me, including one about the big taxidermy bear in the main hall at my sister's university.

There were things from the Sears catalog, too, whose pages I turned greedily from the moment it arrived, but most of those things are long gone, while many of the homemade things are still tucked away in hidden corners of my house.

As spectacular as the gifts always were—and I was too small to appreciate how special they were—it was the fact of Santa—of his having been in the house, sitting in our living room eating cookies, doing magic things with his magic reindeer—that made Christmas so important. I would ponder the room. Did he touch that? Did he sit there? Was there soot on the floor from his boots? He drank from this glass! Was that bump I heard last night the reindeer on the roof?

Eventually, I caught them. I had been suspecting for some time, and the final year was an exercise in pretending I still believed. When I found a price tag on the Monopoly game that Santa was supposed to have brought, I confronted my mother in her big yellow kitchen.

"Do you really want to know?" she asked. I really didn't. With the certainty, I felt genuine despair. I didn't see Santa Claus as a creature of my family's love for me. I only saw a flat, sensible world with no magic in it. It took me years to stop being depressed at Christmas, and I realize now how much my brother's and sister's work to make Christmas for me must have helped them through that bleak transition.

Someone said to me recently that believing in Santa Claus prepares children for a life of faith and mystery—for believing in things you can't see. Maybe that's true. For me, though, the loss of Santa left a little hole in my heart that I still wrestle with. As an almost-grown-up, I have come to see that the world is more beautiful and mysterious than we can know, and in bigger, more staggering ways than Santa Claus. These mysteries are before our eyes if only we see. But just once, it would be wonderful to go back and to know, to really know, that Santa Claus was on the roof.

The Great Unwriting

Writing this morning felt like returning to a workout with stiff muscles and old bones creaking. The words seeped gunk-ily from my brain like sludge from a neglected engine. My focus was squirrel-like, and my capacity for narrative stunted.

It was not like riding a bicycle.

Have I mixed a sufficient number of metaphors?

Nevertheless, my year's hiatus from serious work on my novel had finally reached the point where it no longer felt like a gleeful game of hooky but instead a denial of my existential self. Without writing—without a purpose—the dust, the laundry and daily housework, the empty glasses and bottles of supplements on my nightstand had become the sum of my days. I began to feel I was 107 and waiting to die.

So, even at this stage in life, I've learned something new about myself: depression is a motivator. I've also had to acknowledge that I need to write, which, curiously, I did not know.

Not everyone needs something like this. Some people are fulfilled by the daily realities of routine and loved ones, dinners out, shopping trips, community events, and vacations. I would like to say that I wish I were like that, but I do not. I have this unasked for, and yet fully self-endorsed need to do this one thing. And the need for this one thing is what I had sought as an opera singer and as a teacher, but those things were not *the* thing. For whatever reason, that thing is writing, and if I don't do it, my time on earth is wasted.

I don't know for sure whether I am at last emerging from the doldrums I have been becalmed in. Only time will tell. But something about this feels like a faint breeze in the sails.

I don't think, however, that the time was wasted. I think I needed the Great Unwriting for some reason. It was my long summer in the midst of an academic year. My sabbatical.

What's funny is that you'd think in all that unscheduled, unwriting time I'd have gotten a million other tasks completed: The garden tended, the stones laid, the stone floors scrubbed and sealed, the picket fence at the lake cottage stripped and painted. But the opposite is true. Each task seemed at the time like an obstacle to writing and therefore something not to be attempted. And so, I drifted, untethered to deadlines, or even to my own identity, the days passing, slipping away, lethargy surrounding me like a damp mist. I needed the structure and completion of my writing schedule to liberate me to do the other lesser tasks.

Throughout my life I have felt a continual need to clear my calendar: to create days uninterrupted by external obligation. I have yearned to eradicate appointments, meetings and coffee dates, days at the office. And now, having finally achieved my own nirvana of unscheduled time, I find that my life is curiously featureless, like an uncut diamond.

I still dread the disorder and anxiety of travel. But I want to see the world. I still prefer a day uncluttered by appointments.

But I want to have friends and to leave the house.

There may be a connection between having received the new booster and my renewed enthusiasm to re-engage. I can be curiously out of touch with my own motivations. It doesn't really matter. I can plan my days however I like. But first I have to get up every morning and write.

Rows ✦

I t was pre-dawn, and I had been working for hours. I had just stepped out onto the porch at the house we were renting in Maine and was enjoying the calm when I heard a rhythmic noise. Tock-tock-whoosh, tock-tock-whoosh. I thought at first that it was drops from the eaves after all the rain we'd had, but as it grew louder, I realized it was moving and coming closer. I leaned against the railing and looked out at the lake, waiting for a craft to come into view.

It was a shell with one rower. It was elegantly thin, moving at a great clip, and leaving geometric designs that widened and faded in its wake. The sound of the oars reverberated across the lake. I thought about the rower's early morning, rising to be on the water before the sun rose, and felt a bit of envy at the pleasures of deep exercise, alone, with the sun just hidden behind the mountains at the east side of the water. I rise in the dark, too, but depend on hot coffee—although, perhaps, the same combination of joy and willpower—to sit comfortably on a chair, my legs crossed under me, pressing toward my writing deadline. I count words every morning, gauging my progress. Only two months left.

As he rowed back twenty minutes later, his pace was still strong but just barely slower. Tock-tock-whoosh. The sound rose and fell as he approached, then moved off into the distance, fading into the morning's birdsong.

It was a moment of deep and unexpected beauty.

It's surprising sometimes the things that can make life magical.

Lake Panic ❈

I t's five a.m. I've been up for an hour, working on my book. It was fully dark when I woke, but now I can see the black outlines of the hills across the lake. An owl with an unfamiliar song calls out alone in the dark.

It's not been a productive morning. Yesterday, I sailed … new ideas, new pages, new essay. But today, perhaps distracted by terrors abroad and the prospect of traveling home, I am dry of ideas.

I am often anxious about travel. It's the upheaval, mostly. My stomach is vaguely unsettled. It's pure nerves.

The news does not penetrate here. But I am acutely aware of what is happening on the other side of the world. It is August 31st. The deadline for withdrawal from Afghanistan. Sometimes imagination is not a gift. This, too, gives flavor to my anxiety.

I am sad about leaving this place. I don't love the house, it's true. It's too dark and rickety for my taste. But the lake is beautiful, the wide porches of the house have vistas of water and hills. I like the little town nearby. And my people are here. I love them, and in this pandemic world I have missed them deeply.

I have a dream of being able to swim across the lake at

home. At the beginning of the summer, I searched without
success for a coach to help me build stamina and skill and confidence. I know I am afraid of deep water, but until yesterday, I
had not known the reality of it. I can name it now. It is terror.

The water here is so much different from our lake at
home. For one thing, it's a much bigger place, and there is a
magnificence about it. Instead of marshes along the edges and
a sandy bottom, there are rocks below and hills above. The
length of it is well over a mile. The water is quite cool and
clear; you can sit on the pier and look straight down to the
rocky bottom. It seems so close, as if you could stand on the
bottom and touch the pier.

But yesterday, when I went to swim, I realized too late
how very deep it was. Just off the pier it was already far over
my head, and I clung to the ladder, feeling the deep spasm
of panic in my lungs that I recall from childhood. I spoke to
myself. I was not alone. I tried to calm myself. I would not
drown. But I was not merely afraid. It was deep and primal.
It was only by clinging to a floating device that I could finally
allow myself to let go of the ladder. But I was not soothed by
the experience of floating as I am at home.

I love the water. At home, our lake is small and friendly,
shallow for a long way out. I never need to be in water over
my head. I swim respectable distances, and when I tire, I lie on
my back, floating peacefully. I never touch the bottom, but I
know it's there. Those floats are the highlights of my summers,
and I long for them in winter. There is no good reason for
this panic. Why? I ask myself. What am I half-remembering,
buried deep?

Familiar Lake Michigan—far larger than this and far more dangerous—does not instill this fear in me. I feel respect and awe. It is noisy. Raucous. Its invisible rip currents can lure swimmers to their deaths; its storms have sunken many ships. But it is not a stealthy danger. It is bold, open, and obvious.

This lake has a still beauty that beckons seductively. So calm, so peaceful, so deep, and cool. There was a cold sliding feeling being in that water that I felt in my chest. I felt I could slip deep below the surface, as if hands were waiting to pull me down. The water lured and called to me. I love to swim. I had wanted to be there. I had yearned for it. So why, then, was I so—not just afraid—I felt I was in danger of being possessed by it, of sliding beneath it forever and watching the world slip away from me. The lake had a silky coolness, and I felt the shivers begin to shake me from the core of my body. Across the world, even now, the Taliban begins its task of killing. Is this what that fear is like? This deep, inner convulsion?

The owl has travelled, and its call is much fainter now. Perhaps there is another one, too, replying. I can't tell. The east is pale yellow, and the southern sky is pink with deep blue gray streaks of clouds. The lake is a pale blue, calm and still.

Now I can see the outlines of the columns and the chairs on the porch. Upstairs, the baby gives one cry and sleeps again. Soon the three-year-old sleeping in the next room will wander in drowsily, asking for various kinds of help, then snuggling against me in the silence of the house. She's been told by her parents not to disturb me in the mornings, but I can't send her away, not knowing, in this pandemic world, when I will see her again.

The End of Everything

I am home. It is a balmy, beautiful August morning. I sit drinking coffee by our lake, the dogs around me. Elderly Pete basks peacefully in the sun. Auggie snorts impatiently, waiting for me to engage with his ball-playing, and young Eli has left his watch post at the end of the dock to lie next to my chair. A lawn mower purrs in the distance. A door slams. Fish jump. Ducks quack and splash. Squirrels chatter. Birds call. A bull frog grumps.

All should be well.

But across the world, chaos reigns. Death, destruction, fear, murder, torture, rape, and slavery threaten. People climb onto departing airplanes, clinging to the wings, in desperate fear of what is to come. The planes depart, and the bodies can be seen hurtling to earth, prey to the most horrific final fears as they fall.

An American flag flutters in the breeze across the lake.

Here, there is comfort in powerlessness. With no recourse but to drink my coffee, I can stay comfortable. I can't fix Afghanistan. I can't save a single person. Lucky me.

I am ashamed.

And yet … and yet … this day, this calm, this comfort, this stroke of fate that brought me here, to have been born in a free state, in a liberal democracy … this is fortune. And to leave it unnoticed, to ignore it, not to savor it, is the very definition of sin.

I envy my dogs in their innocence.

There are no clouds in the sky, but there is a cloud over this day.

May God forgive us.

Pete's Last Days ❖

When our dog, Pete, died, he was mourned by tens of thousands of people around the world. One elderly gentleman from South America built a household shrine to him; artists sent portraits of him; strangers made donations in his name to animal shelters across the United States and Canada. For two days, RIP Pete was trending across Twitter in the United States. His obituary had more than five million views. It was not a predictable ending for a little dog rescued from a kill shelter.

We got Pete in the chaos following Hurricane Katrina in 2005. A story in the local paper announced the arrival of Katrina rescues in our area, and I called immediately. "They've all been adopted already, but we have some other lovely dogs …"

I went to their website and promptly landed at the photo of a young hound dog with a sad little face. "Bobbie. Sweet," it said. He was supposedly a greyhound mix, but while we never doubted he was a coursing hound, it's more likely that there was whippet in him rather than greyhound. The foster family guessed he was about ten months old and told us he had been abused, had been part of a litter of eleven puppies, and had lived in a small cage. He'd been rescued from a kill shelter in Indiana. We were also told he had been thrown.

We brought our golden retriever, Reggie, to meet him, and they got along fine, so Bobbie came home with us, and we began the long drive home from western Wisconsin.

We were introduced immediately to the distinctions between hound dogs and retrievers. When we stopped on the way home and went, briefly, inside a store, I left my taco salad on the dashboard. Accustomed to the docile good behavior of Reggie, it never occurred to me that this was a bad idea. When we returned a few minutes later, the paper wrapper sat intact on the dashboard, licked clean. There was no crumb left. Both dogs gazed back at us, innocent-eyed, but we knew who had eaten the taco salad. We looked at each other and laughed, but I felt some trepidation. Life was going to be different in ways I hadn't considered.

Our young sons met our new dog, and we discussed his name. We already had a family member named Bob, so we felt a change was in order. They chose "Peter." My father and mother came to meet him, and Pete immediately worked his charms on them both. "He's a lovely addition to the family," my father said as Pete nudged his hand asking for love.

Pete's history of abuse was clear in multiple ways. In his early time with us, when anyone moved suddenly toward him, he would roll on his back and pee submissively; a sudden hand movement, and he would flinch. But more interesting, he had learned manipulation, and he used his considerable wit to charm and ingratiate. Had he been able to speak, his first words would have been, "That's a lovely dress you're wearing, Mrs. Cleaver."

Pete's big puppy dog eyes are what made him famous on Twitter, but his personality was far more complex. He was not always sweet. In fact, he was more of a curmudgeon than his fans ever fully understood. Early photos of Pete—he was terrified of cameras—show a grumpy dog with a face like a man in a hostage situation. People often ask if we have puppy photos of Pete, but aside from the fact that he was almost full-grown when he came to us, he actually used to run and hide if a camera came out. My husband's theory is that someone once took an unflattering photo of him. It wasn't until phone cameras were in general use that we were able to take his photo without traumatizing him.

Pete went to obedience training and learned all the basics, but when the class turned to Canine Good Citizenship training, with dropped books, whistles, wheelchairs, and other surprises, Pete cowered and trembled. We took him home. Pete's imperfect standards of citizenship would have to suffice.

As a young dog, Pete was naughty. He barked incessantly. He ran away. And when he ran, he was a thing of beauty. His speed and grace were astonishing. He leapt like a deer, effortlessly and with perfect form. He was also both standoffish, and a deep cuddler. At night he would sneak off downstairs to our library couch to sleep alone, but he would nap with me in the afternoons, his face lying against mine.

The balance of our two-dog pack remained stable for some time. Pete joined Reggie, and when Reggie succumbed to lymphoma, Moses joined Pete. That was when Pete moved into the alpha position (after us, of course). As Pete aged, however, around ten, we began to notice that his hearing was failing. One morning, as I watched from twenty feet away, a coyote appeared and began stalking Pete without him knowing.

Before I could move or shout, Moses was there, chasing the coyote off, but leaving Pete unprotected. That was when I realized that we needed a second German Shepherd. Not because three dogs were an ideal number for the household, but because Pete needed a team of guardians. When Auggie finally arrived, and then, ultimately, Eli, Pete looked upon the newcomers with a mixture of resignation and disdain, but he ruled over his pack of enormous shepherds with an iron paw. Even fierce Moses respected Pete's leadership, although he was much bigger and stronger than Pete.

At seventeen years old, Pete was an old dog. Usually, such great ages are reserved for very small dogs, but Pete had always been a good-sized medium, his weight ranging from a hefty 68 pounds to a more fit 58 in his later years. Like all hounds, he loved to eat, and he wasn't particularly fussy. At one point, when we imposed a weight-loss diet he didn't approve, Pete helped himself to carcasses he found in the woods, coming home with blood on his muzzle and some rather ferocious tummy troubles.

We always joked that he had nine lives like a cat. There was the time when, in an alpha correction of young Moses, who was, by then, 130 pounds, Moses fell on Pete, leaving Pete with a hideous Joe Theismann-style injury. Pete was screaming, and it occurred to my distraught husband that this was the kind of thing for which some people would shoot a dog. Instead, with the help of a steady friend, my husband got Pete into the car and raced to the veterinary emergency room. Pete wore a splint for weeks, but nothing could stop him from climbing the stairs to his preferred sleeping spot. The vet chastised us, but I am convinced that putting weight on that leg helped him heal. Pete knew best.

Many years later, we took a listless and chubby Pete to the vet, where we discovered that it wasn't that his thyroid levels were low, it was that he had *no* thyroid levels. The medications made a difference in a matter of days.

On another routine trip to the vet, when Pete was about twelve, we were told that he had beginning stage kidney failure. The best we could do would be to manage it, there was no reversal possible. We took him to a holistic vet nearby, who told us his arthritis medicine might be the culprit and prescribed a homemade diet with herbal supplements. Within weeks, friends were commenting on how different Pete seemed: lively, youthful, and slim. Within two months, tests showed his kidney function was back to normal.

Pete lived out his seniority as he had lived out his youth: independent, grumpy, and self-directed. But in a household where he had always been the smallest dog, he used his hound dog eyes to get what he wanted from his people and ensconced himself firmly in the alpha position with his pack mates. We encouraged this, knowing it was better for Moses not to get any big ideas. Three German Shepherds later, Pete was alpha to the end, in his last week, snarling and biting Auggie on the leg for some infraction of etiquette.

Two months before his death, we took Pete in to have some soft tissue growths removed. We knew they were cancerous, and we had decided, with our vet, that the threat of painful necrotic ruptures was worse than the dangers of surgery. Within twenty minutes of dropping him off, I got a call. They had x-rayed Pete's lungs, and they were full of tumors.

Surgery was impossible.

"Take him home and love him while you can," we were told.

The next morning, I was engrossed in work when I suddenly realized the dogs were nowhere to be seen. I went all around the house looking out the windows and then went to the door and whistled. My dogs know that whistle is the ultimate summons, and they always come running. I heard no responding movement in the woods. Alarmed, I whistled again and, barefoot, ran down our long driveway toward the road. I looked to the left, and there was Auggie, running full speed from all the way down the road. Behind him lumbered young Eli, who, despite being built like a truck, is quite speedy. And behind him, running at top speed (although not as fast as formerly), ears flapping and tongue lolling, lungs full of tumors, came Pete, the alpha, the incitement artist, the leader of all naughty adventures. My dogs rarely leave our property, and they hadn't in years. But Pete's eyes were sparkling with delight, and I have no doubt who had led my obedient German Shepherds astray.

Pete's end came suddenly after a happy day in the sun and a dinner of roast chicken. Eli, alert to Pete's distress, crawled under the bushes to be with him and licked his face. The ride to the vet was horrifying, but by the time we got Pete to the emergency room, he was nearly gone. He died in my husband's arms.

I really don't think death can be much better than that. I believe—I hope—that in Pete's last moments he knew how much he was loved. Pete was, after all, the ultimate winner in the dog lottery of life.

For Jeff and Sahar ✤

Anyone can fall in love. And most of us who have been married will acknowledge that it helps if love is the first requirement. The ancient vows that Sahar and Jeff are about to make confirm it: we promise first "to love."

But, as we here make a commitment to support Sahar and Jeff in their marriage, we understand that love is not enough. I want to say "mere" love, although that would be at odds with every philosophy and theology in the world. But love can be a fleeting emotion. That's why when we experience real love, most civilizations suggest that we add something more. We want to vow that our commitment is forever and that we mean more than only how we feel.

Love, Honor, Comfort, and Keep. They are ancient poetic words, and they bear testament to an essential truth: marriage is hard.

It would seem at first thought that in the commitment that they are making today, the challenges Sahar and Jeff face will be accelerated by their different cultural heritages. But this is only a detail. Because in many ways every marriage is a melding of cultures … of family … of values … of male and female.

Our work, as married people, is to accept the alien nature of the other. And, come to think of it, isn't that the work of us all?

Because the fundamental requirements of all human relationships are those we practice first at home, and so, the relationship of husband and wife reflects our relationship with the whole world. That is not a coincidence.

We start with the imperative to love, with all that it entails, but there are also these other requirements:

Honor.

Comfort.

Keep.

Together, they form a hierarchy, with each of these actions dependent upon the other.

Honoring ... it means we don't hold one another in contempt ... that our familiarity breeds, instead, respect, and generosity, and patience, and understanding.

And we cannot comfort without honoring, because offering comfort requires an essential respect of our beloved's individual humanity and need.

Comfort requires, too, understanding the value of offering not what *we* need, but what *someone else* needs—which is almost never the same thing.

Comfort is an act of solidarity but also an act of empathy— a moving out of ourselves and our needs and into the needs of someone else.

If I need solitude, maybe I need to understand that at the same moment, my partner needs affection. And the efforts we make to frame the world based on someone else's needs is key part of marriage and, indeed, of any relationship.

And "keep." What does that mean? We keep watch; we keep time; we keep chickens.

But to keep one another …

It's vigilance, isn't it. It means we hold one another in esteem, with honor. We comfort. *We pay attention.* Sometimes at a cost to ourselves and our pressing priorities. But … it also means to give shelter. We smooth paths … we encourage … we understand foibles … we attempt to care, not just for physical but for emotional requirements.

Come to think of it, it is a bit like chickens.

We nurture.

We protect.

We *keep.*

Which brings us back to love. These vows are all encompassed in the act of loving; they are the recipe for all human relationships. To Love, Honor, Comfort, and Keep.

It is more than a philosophy. It is an action, an endeavor, our daily work. And it is a challenge.

A healthy marriage—the keeping of these vows—requires fierce dedication, determination, and commitment, all entered into in the endeavor of love.

Sometimes blindly, sometimes fervently. But deliberately, reverently, joyfully, and not just with our whole hearts, but with every fiber of our beings.

From my role as officiant at their wedding in Istanbul.

✦ *Landmarks*

Rose was probably the first non-family adult I ever knew. She would have been thirty when I was born—considerably younger than my mother. But they were best friends. When my family moved away, their friendship remained, and I have written elsewhere about the detailed and frequent correspondence they kept up as records of both our families' lives—my mother's letters scrawled across grocery store notebook paper, Rose's typed at the office in the early hours before the start of business.

Years later, through an act of generosity, I got to know Rose's twin sister, Evelyn. She opened her New York home to me when I was traveling there weekly to audition for opera roles during the hemorrhaging money phase of my career. I slept on the futon in her living room and brought flowers, wine, or chocolate in appreciation.

My family's stories of Rose and Evelyn rise to the stuff of legend. My mother never learned to drive, and during the early years of their friendship, she and Rose went everywhere together with me toddling along. Rose was tall; my mother was four foot eleven. And a half. Both were outspoken, energetic women, but even my mother did not have Rose's confidence, and occasionally my mother, who never thought she deserved very much, was a bit uncomfortable with her friend's defense of her. There were the times Rose would speak up to urge a store clerk to wait on my mother, who was somewhat hidden behind the high counter: "This lady here is next! She's been waiting longer than anyone else!" In stores, if a correct size were not in sight, Rose would open the hidden bins beneath the sales counter to sort through the backstock while my mother hung back. After waiting for a break in traffic, unable to pull out of a parking lot, Rose would declare; "I'm just going to lean on my horn and go."

Rose was widowed young, but I never saw her grief. She carried on in her force of nature way, living in the New Jersey bedroom community that is my hometown, spending summers in Vermont, and working occasionally as an executive secretary, although I doubt she needed to.

Evelyn was both divorced and widowed, but one of her husbands was the love of her life. She lived most of her life in New York, working at a foundation and later at a publishing house. Both women wrote poetry and won awards for it. I think my mother was not particularly appreciative when Rose sent her work, but my mother wasn't interested in poetry. When I read them, however, I see depth and talent.

Now, I am a grandmother. My mother is long gone. But Rose and Evelyn are ninety-one, closing fast on ninety-two, and I am on a much-delayed trip to New York and New Jersey to see them. COVID delayed me several years, so I missed the opportunity to go back to my childhood neighborhood, because Rose has since sold her house and moved to assisted living. Evelyn, who planned for a city retirement, lives in the same place she's been in for thirty years, a first floor Manhattan apartment within walking distance of Lincoln Center. Both tell me they are failing.

So, I have packed for a few days' trip. Tomorrow I will meet Evelyn at her apartment, and together we will take a car to New Jersey to have lunch with Rose. I have brought a stainless-steel cocktail shaker and ice strainer (curiously resembling a bomb and carried in a shopping bag in case they should attract the attention of the TSA), and a tiny bottle of artisanal bitters to make them their favorite Manhattans. We will all spend the day together. On the second day, I will go to Evelyn's apartment, and have offered my services to do any little things she may need.

My flight is early this morning, and I am watching the red glow of the sunrise as we fly east. The flurry of preparations and planning have permitted me to avoid thinking about the meaning of this trip until now. I sit holding airline coffee and looking out the airplane window at the black earth below. I know the route well, and even in the dark I recognize certain landmarks. These two women have been landmarks, too: a constant presence in my life, sometimes near and sometimes far. I have long since lost the older generation of my family, as has my husband, and we stand now, together, on the precipice of mortality, not—I hope—quite against the edge. Yet these two indomitable women—smart, funny, audacious, fast-talking, and often laughing—are still here, essentially unchanged. There are few things in life so constant.

And so, this trip will be a tribute, but I hope not a farewell. I really don't like to contemplate the prospect of a world without them.

Adventures in Travel: Part Deux

We rented a car on a recent trip to France. We were going to visit our daughter and two grandsons, so even though large cars in Europe are a genuine inconvenience on narrow, ancient streets—and somewhat embarrassing in an ugly American kind of way—we had to have something that would accommodate five.

The car was brand new. A hybrid. All fine. But leaving aside the fact that it handled like a hot air balloon, and that despite its size could barely fit our two suitcases in the back, it had another, more serious flaw. I refer to the alarms.

I continue to be astonished by the direction that safety engineers have taken. I wonder whether any of them actually drive their own inventions and find them helpful, or whether, perhaps, they think everyone else is an idiot. Or possibly, they are the types of people who have low excitability levels and require extreme measures to shake them out of a natural torpor. In any case, it didn't take long for us to discover that this car had audible safety alarms permanently set to Hysteria.

Years of marriage have taught us to stay with our respective strong suits when dividing labor. I love cars and am a relatively happy and calm driver but cannot read a map. My husband is good at navigation. So, when we are traveling in Europe, I am almost always the one behind the wheel. It took about ten minutes to discover that this particular vehicle did not have a height adjustment for the seat, so no matter how we tried, I was unable to see completely over the hood. I now realize this is because the experts who designed the car had decided that the driver needn't see because the car would simply terrify her into the safest path. After my husband had gotten the sitting on a phone book jokes out of his system, we set off.

As we pulled up to the rental company gate to insert the exit ticket, the car began a high-pitched beeping that made us both jump. The "there's something close to the car" beep had two tones—one for the danger in front (the gate) and another for the danger to the side (the ticket machine). The level of pitch and volume seemed more appropriate to the Titanic hitting an iceberg, and the clamor continued for as long as we were stopped. It took several minutes for my heart rate to go down. Perhaps it was so startling because we were not used to the car, we thought.

But, no.

It was dark. And snowing. I was driving an unfamiliar car after twenty-four hours of travel, searching for a route I had only driven a few times many years before. It was rush hour, and the French driving style is … assertive. The GPS was curiously silent, but I was headed toward a roundabout which would require some decision making. Suddenly, in the dark, a woman's voice seemed to come from the back seat. "DANGER ZONE!" she announced. "DANGER ZONE!" We both jumped, and I nearly swerved. The car beeped hideously. The dashboard flashed red.

"Jesus Christ!" I said, calmly.

"What the hell was that?!" my husband replied.

Traffic swirled around us, merging and weaving as the cars chose their exits at top speed, changing lanes in front and behind us with hair-raising aggression.

"Go that way!!"

"What way?"

"THAT way! Quick! Get over! Right! Right!! RIGHT!!!"

My husband's voice of alarm was considerably less unsettling than the car's.

We exited the roundabout as a small panel truck darted in front of us with inches to spare. There were no alarms for that.

We drove on. I tried not to clench the wheel.

"What should I do after this?" I asked my exhausted husband. He gestured vaguely in a direction.

"I can't see your hand while I'm driving," I said, somewhat testily.

"DANGER ZONE!" Announced the car, accompanied by a choir of beeping and flashing red lights.

"You missed the turn."

"How was I supposed to tell? It was very confusing."

There then followed a lively marital exchange of views, culminating in the predictable, "Well, why don't you drive then."

We approached another roundabout. "DANGER ZONE!" said the woman in the back seat with alarms and flashing lights. "DANGER ZONE!"

Like much of Europe, the French traffic system depends

less upon stop lights than upon roundabouts for intersections. There were lots of them, approximately one city block apart, sometimes more frequent, all accompanied by the relentless alarm system. "DANGER ZONE!"

I confess that my initial entries to the roundabouts were somewhat trepidatious, mainly because I wasn't accustomed to the cumbersome car, but also because the French habit of darting in and around was happening at a more lively pace than that of most American drivers. It's distracting to be screamed at while trying to calmly merge with high-speed traffic coming from multiple angles, and the DANGER ZONE alarms were beginning to unnerve me.

After twenty minutes of dodging and weaving through traffic, we found the main road. "DANGER ZONE!" announced the alarm system as we merged. "DANGER ZONE!"

As we entered the highway—a major commercial route running to and from Paris and the south—I soon realized that speed was not a friend to this particular vehicle. It bobbled dangerously as I approached the 130 kph speed limit, but when I slowed down to accommodate it, other drivers sped up to the very limit of the bumper, pressuring me to move faster. There were hundreds of the super-sized *camions* common in the EU, and despite the snow, none of them showed an inclination to slow down. There were no plows and no salt trucks. Slush was accumulating on the road. I silently pondered the potential irony of whether this trip to see our family would end in our deaths and not from COVID.

We had about 90 kilometers to go, and, with the help of

familiar music on the Bluetooth system, gradually we settled into the routine of the traffic and a less frantic—if deeply fatigued and slightly desperate—state of mind. Nevertheless, the speed and number of trucks on the road, and the worsening road conditions did not encourage calm.

We had crossed the Aquitaine and the Dordogne rivers, and after a long incline, we began to go downhill. As I eased off on the accelerator, a bell began to ring, and a new light began to flash on the dashboard. My first thought was some kind of dire engine failure, and my heart sank. But no sooner had I determined we needed to find an exit, than the alarm stopped, and all was calm. Throughout that long drive, this particular set of bells went off half a dozen times, each time rousing an instinctive nervous reaction: what was wrong with the car?

I never did completely figure out what that alarm was for—although it went off occasionally throughout the ten days, always when going downhill. Alarms without explanation are not particularly effective. At one point, when the car fish-tailed in the snow, the dashboard flashed a red coffee cup, helpfully suggesting I pull off the road for a rest. There was also a flashing red speed limit light when I was going too fast (difficult to avoid when a large truck's grill fills your rear-view mirror) or too slow (because the pavement was slippery, and I have judgement, which, apparently, the safety engineers did not expect). I would suggest to the engineers that a flashing red light in your field of vision is not what you need when navigating a tricky situation. At last, we saw the exit ahead, and I signaled to take the right turn. "DANGER ZONE!" shrieked the car.

We reached our destination, at last, without mishap—unless, of course, you count the alarms—and settled into a lovely, long visit. We spent most of our time at home, making a cozy Christmas, walking the dog, playing games, watching movies, and constructing IKEA systems.

But we did find time for a day trip to the ancient town of Perigueux. It was the busy week before Christmas, and there was no parking available on the streets. Our drive into the parking garage was harrowing, our car barely fitting in the narrow ramps that spiraled into the bowels of the garage. We slowly found our way through two levels as the car merrily called "DANGER ZONE!" and beeped without stopping. The walls were too close, apparently. "DANGER ZONE!"

Fed up after several days, we spent twenty minutes trying to find a way to turn off the alarms, but our only option was to be yelled at by a male, rather than a female voice. I found myself fantasizing about Stanley Kubrick's death of Hal scene.

The alarm system became a recurring topic of conversation on family outings. I confess it was helpful in parking on the narrow streets, despite its caution levels being set to extremes. Ultimately, we bowed to the inevitable, and reached an uneasy détente with the car.

By the end of the ten-day visit, however, full-on screaming struck us all as moderately less distracting than the mechanical alarms and rather more fun. We experimented with the simple—calling out "DANGER ZONE!" at intervals, alternating with the full panic, horror film-style screams. Driving through the bucolic French countryside with all of us periodically yelling in unison—usually as we approached a roundabout—I began to feel we were among the Niebelungen in a Wagnerian opera.

I kind of wish we had captured it on camera, actually.

As we returned the car to the rental agency, I commented to my husband that the alarms made this a car we would never buy. It occurred to us both that what the engineers really needed was warning system for potential buyers. Its deployment would be a welcome consumer service.

❖ *For Jean*

Fall is late this year. It is already mid-October, but for the first time the woods have a tinge of gold just beginning, and the sunlight's yellow is intensified when it shines through the trees. These are the kinds of days I count as finite in my life. All our days are finite, of course, but some seem to belong in a category as different as a gemstone to a handsome pebble.

Life hasn't seemed, really, to have returned to normal for us. The contagion levels are still high where we live, so although we have traveled a bit, and tentatively dined outdoors a few times—enjoying it thoroughly—the cold weather will end that small bit of normality. The world feels smaller.

In pre-COVID times, I would go now to the Island. It is one of the places where the golden light of fall permeates everything. The long, empty roads mean I can walk for miles without seeing a car, and the dogs, who return to me instantly when I call, can run off-leash. We wander through golden lanes, and my brain, usually obsessively plotting and exhausted by the extraction of writing, is distracted by the resonating vibrancy of the color. I remember these walks repeatedly, and return to them in my dreams, and in my books. They are, I think, how I would spend eternity if I could.

But we are mistaken if the wet days, the bleak and dreary ones, are not treasured, too. My dogs, who love to swim but hate the rain, nevertheless run joyfully through wet weeds and brush, shaking themselves with vigor when they come in, smelling of mud. Dogs have a capacity for appreciation that my ideal self would try to emulate, but I am not a dog, and I can't seem to achieve their purity of mind.

My joy ebbs and flows with the seasons. I have never fully understood spring, with its mud, its dirty snow piles, its cold rains, and disappointed hopes. My joy comes when the fall is at its peak, and even still later, with the stark, purple cold of winter. Once the leaves and crops are stripped away, the sculptural lines of the trees and the shape of the earth is revealed, and the light pours down, undiffused. The world seems a brighter, clearer, purer place. That cold clarity purifies me.

In our mortality, I wonder whether there is, too, a clarity that comes as we can, at last, see the end. There is no need for the extraneous, just the focus of comfort, where we can; of love, if we are blessed with it; and the firm hope that when the seasons pass, the essence of what we are will always be.

J.F. Riordan and Moses. Photo by Patrick Manning Photograph

Award-winning author J.F. Riordan has been called "a latter-day Jane Austen." Her mesmerizing literary fiction makes the Great Lakes region one of the characters in a continuing series. The North of the Tension Line books (*North of the Tension Line*; *The Audacity of Goats*; *Robert's Rules*; *A Small Earnest Question*; and soon, *Throwing Bears for George*) represent a sensibility that is distinctively Midwestern, even though the small town politics and gossip will be universally familiar. Riordan celebrates the well-lived life of the ordinary man and woman with meticulously drawn characters and intriguing plots that magnify the beauty and mystery lingering near the surface of everyday life.

Equally adept as an essayist, her writings are by turns insightful and personal; soulful and humorous, and belong at the bedside of anyone in search of the comfort and companionship of a humane voice. She lives in Wisconsin with her husband and two German Shepherds.